P9-BJA-842

the rise of the cultural consumer—
and what it means to your business

Ren

RENAISSANCE
GENERATION

Gen

patricia martin

**PLATINUM
PRESS®**

avon, massachusetts

The Platinum Press® is a registered trademark of F+W Publications, Inc.

Published by Adams Media,
an F+W Publications Company
57 Littlefield Street
Avon, MA 02322
www.adamsmedia.com

ISBN-10: 1-59869-134-1
ISBN-13: 978-1-59869-134-4

Library of Congress Cataloging-in-Publication Data

Martin, Patricia
RenGen / Patricia Martin.
p.   cm.
Includes bibliographical references and index.
ISBN-13: 978-1-59869-134-4 (hardcover)
ISBN-10: 1-59869-134-1 (hardcover)
1. Information society—Economic aspects. 2. Popular culture—Economic
aspects. 3. Marketing—Forecasting. 4. Social change. I. Title.
HM851.M375 2007
306.301'12—dc22   2007003078

Printed in the United States of America.
J I H G F E D C B A

This book is available at quantity discounts for bulk purchases.
For information, please call 1-800-289-0963.

To my family

Contents

Acknowledgments

This book owes a debt to many people who collaborated on shaping its direction. Since I coaxed insights from people all across the United States, I am grateful to a swath of people from all walks of life.

First, I must thank my children, Grace and Emmet, who by now have grown accustomed to seeing their mother typing into the night and have yet to carp about it. They eagerly entertained my questions and theories, especially those regarding youth culture. Without hesitation they gave me access to their friends who were young artists, poets, and online gamers. I owe special thanks to my son Emmet, who made good on the family's investment in a prep school education by diligently fact-checking and proofreading on otherwise gorgeous summer days. To their father, Patrick Penney, I am grateful for his insistence that I pursue my wildest dreams.

My research team earned my undying gratitude. I can't imagine a more persistent associate than Professor Donna Surges Tatum from the University of Chicago. She kept me swimming in the deep end of the pool along with her associates Kay and Johnna, who helped compile data. Alice Sneary rode shotgun through the entire "second cities" research. She attacked research and conducted interviews with gregarious good cheer that made that chapter sing. While on sabbatical from SPSS Corp, Ann Trampas gathered research early in the book's development that proved immensely valuable. And thanks to my public librarian, Betty Laliberte, who scoured library data bases around the world on my behalf.

Throughout the writing of this book, I never lacked for great minds to help me wrestle insights out of data. Alane Wilson from OCLC offered well-researched perspectives on user trends in libraries. My clients Lisa Key from the Art Institute and Sandra Davis of the Seattle Opera connected me with hard-to-reach influentials. Que Gaskins from Reebok distinguished himself with valor for bravely embracing RenGen theory early. Jim Newcomb at Boeing gave me his thoughts even when his schedule didn't permit it. Market researcher Carol White decoded data and kept straight the weaving of facts into theories. Peggy Barber kept her mind and her Rolodex open; both of them proved golden resources. Marj Halperin opened the door to a cadre of female RenGen who taught me new approaches to old problems. I am also grateful to Randy Cohen and Bob Lynch from Americans for the Arts for tending to the big picture.

I presented various chapters of the book to outside readers who labored over them and sent lengthy e-mails with feedback. Bonnie Bachman, John Becker, Jeff Borden, Jay Kelly, Carla Williams, and Susan Rosetti all deserve my gratitude for tramping through the early versions of the book. In particular, my friend and colleague Margaret Monsour saved the people at Adams Media from some frightful early versions.

Carol Rosenthal kept my writing honest. No matter how often I veered into overblown prose she whittled me down to size, and the book is better for it. Jill Alexander, my editor at Adams Media, contributed immensely to the book's organization, but more important, she believed in the idea of the book from the get-go. Bob Reed from *Bloomberg* chipped in with advice at critical moments. My understanding of the RenGen aesthetic was aided by the keen insights of magazine designers Mary K. Baumann and Will Hopkins. Downright bloodhounds of emerging visual trends, they unearthed one hot trend after another and arrayed them before me, to my deepest gratitude. Professor Robert Roemer led me through Rome's treasures including a private viewing of the Sistine Chapel, where I spent a dizzying few hours.

Thanks to my dear friends Jennifer Alesi and Francesca Pignataro. Jennifer for making a cameo appearance in the book and Francesca, the savvy restaurateur, for her insights into dining trends.

To my trusted agent, Diane Nine, I am grateful for her mentorship and faith in me. To my lawyer, Mary Hutchings Reed who is herself a renaissance woman, I am also grateful. In writing this book, as in my everyday life as a consultant, I am blessed to have extraordinary clients. They patiently awaited my return to the office and seemed genuinely excited that I was running the intellectual equivalent of a marathon. Thank you.

Introduction

Three years ago, while making my way through the snarl of early morning traffic, I snapped on the radio to hear that a popular writer, David Sedaris, was coming to Chicago. I should call for tickets, I thought. But I got busy and didn't remember until a day later. And by then the event was sold out.

"What? But he's a writer!" I argued with the box-office assistant on the other end of the phone. I pressed further, "How many seats are in that auditorium?" Five thousand, she told me. Over lunch later that week, I recounted the story to a friend who is a concert promoter. What kind of person sells out a 5,000-seat auditorium overnight in a major city? My friend smiled knowingly. "A rock star," he said.

That crescendo moment was one in a series of occurrences that struck me as odd because it challenged what I thought I understood about mainstream interests. The mass market in America has been defined by reality television and fast food. The common perception is that Americans, overfed and undereducated, respond only to the simplest ideas. The typical American is also seen as seeking out leisure activities that are passive, unchallenging, and devoid of any intellectual content. After a few years of working with professionals in the entertainment, media, and marketing industries, I had subtly surrendered to their frequent bromides that the average Joe in America is, well, below average.

This book challenges that assumption.

Because, if it were true, why do 65 percent of Americans cite reading as their preferred leisure activity? Why do companies like Google™ and Microsoft® seek to borrow from the intellectual sanctums of museums and libraries for entertainment content? Why do art museums, aquariums, zoos, and science centers draw more foot traffic than all the professional sports teams in the United States combined, including auto racing? Why do teenagers turn up in record numbers to poetry slams and post original short stories on their blogs? Why have applications to art schools shown aggressive growth over the last decade? Why does author David Sedaris fill venues large enough to host bands like Green Day?

Here is my assessment: Mass market tastes and aspirations are shifting gears in the knowledge society. If 65 percent of American households read for pleasure and attend an average of three cultural events per year, and they state a belief that exposure to the arts is good for their kids, then this is no cultural wasteland. I studied the audiences who appreciate independent film, literary art, music from classical to hip-hop, visual art and live theater. My research revealed a single, common denominator across all thirteen cities we looked at, from Anchorage to Pittsburgh, Cleveland to Chicago: people who value these experiences also value learning. To put it another way, more and more people enjoy a lively life of the mind and seek ways to express it.

This book makes one truth clear: a new social order is emerging based on a more enlightened sensibility. A growing stratum of the public is preparing to begin a second renaissance. The evidence of its emergence abounds. But, without clear grounding in an updated view of the society in which we live, raise our kids, and work, our economy will fail to benefit from this new wave of opportunity.

The David Sedaris event inspired me to set out on a journey to discover the source of this undercurrent that turns an artist into a popular culture phenom. To help me, I recruited two researchers and several advisors and embarked on a two-year process to better understand what I was witnessing. Before long, I was engaging colleagues, friends, even my children, in theorizing and testing assumptions. My theories developed organically, looping from data to assumptions to debate and revision, all with the help of everyday people.

In the spring of 2004, I reached a crossroads. During a four-hour delay in the Philadelphia airport I went to the bar, ordered a drink, and reached into my briefcase for my research notepad. It wasn't there. In a frenzy, I groped through the bag, front pocket, side pocket, inside pocket. Nothing. Weeks of observations lost.

At that moment I pledged to dedicate myself to the research. I opened my planner to carve entire weeks out of my calendar, but when I turned the page to August, there were three weeks with a red line marked "trip to Rome." Nearly a year before, I had committed to fulfill a long-held promise to myself to visit the eternal city. But at that moment in the Philadelphia airport, it was an exasperating prospect for a diversion I could ill afford. However, the trip to Rome proved to be pivotal to the writing of this book.

In the heat and dust of the Roman summer, I began to see beyond the ruins—beyond the ornate relics of the once imperial

Catholic Church, beyond the masterworks by great artists never since matched in creative output on such a scale, to see clearly one question: What made this all possible? In trying to answer that question, something clicked. That level of mastery occurs for a reason; it is not a fluke. What I would later discover went beyond the usual notions of a renaissance as the confluence of talent, ideas, sponsorship, and an appreciative public. This book is not about the Renaissance, per se, it is about the question: What forces bring about a renaissance? This book seeks to answer that question.

For the next year, I delved into history books, consulted scholars, educators, marketers, business people, artists, psychologists, physicians, scientists, urban planners, and even futurists. I went back and forth across time periods and geography to discover the social, political, and economic patterns that lead to a renaissance.

In my professional life as a consultant, I work with people in a world where the arts, business, education, and entertainment converge. Previously, these sectors had little interaction. But the Internet has changed that, and the dividers between disciplines have become increasingly permeable. Having pioneered a career as a marketing specialist in a fast-growing discipline of edutainment, I am invited to speak a lot. As a matter of necessity, I made my talks part of the organic process of this book. Once I coined the term *RenGen,* short for *renaissance generation,* I began talking about it in speeches across the country. Some writers would consider this risky, since you expose your precious intellectual property to potential theft. However, it provided me with a powerful weapon. It enabled me to recruit culture scouts—people who had also picked up the scent on the trail and were willing to share their observations.

And recruit I did. Theater ushers, schoolteachers, clerks at my local store, librarians, high schoolers, and an online game developer, were all potential scouts. I expanded my notions of "culture" to embrace a broad swath of perspectives. I began calling it the Tocqueville method, borrowed from the nineteenth-century French nobleman who, in his mid-twenties, traveled the breadth of Jacksonian America to investigate the social and political effects of democracy to predict what might come after the revolution in his homeland.

Later, a variety of methods were added to gather the information that led to this book. Major foundations were sources for research. The Wallace Foundation unlocked their vault of public opinion research and allowed me to feast on their findings. The New York Philharmonic furnished a stack of audience surveys that stood six inches high on my desk. In the business community, one contact led to another, and I found myself talking with research directors and analysts who generously shared their data and perspectives on the shifts they were seeing in consumer values.

With my office a slalom course of piles, I knew I needed some structure. I signed up for a communications course at the University of Chicago's Graham School for executives needing to convey scientific data in everyday presentations. The course was taught by Donna Tatum, an instructor in communications and a psychometrician. Her academic specialty involves measuring intelligence, personality, and belief systems as they relate to human performance. The scientific measurement of unobservable phenomena is difficult, but Professor Tatum had specific wisdom about how to assess and interpret subtle social phenomena. She proved to be exceptionally personable, and her insights were invaluable. Intrigued by my theory, she became an active collaborator.

Working with Donna Tatum's team, we embarked on original research consisting of an online survey taken from a global pool of 1,400 senior marketing executives. We tested to see how aware they were of the phenomenon we were tracking. Better yet, we tested to see if they were acting on it. Simultaneously, we gathered insights from 30 recognized experts in marketing, entertainment, performing arts, art schools, museums, and libraries.

Out of this process, I emerged convinced that the past fifty years of American life is not an endless downward spiral—it is a prelude. In fact, it looks a lot like what happens right before a renaissance.

CHAPTER ONE

Preconditions for a Rebirth

This book is about the rise of the next renaissance generation—the *RenGen*—an emerging strata of enlightened individuals who are hungry for ideas and ways to express them. It also refers to a cultural movement that is being created by the confluence of art, science, education, popular entertainment, and business. The Renaissance of the fifteenth century was a flowering of civilization—a "rebirth" of art, scientific invention, culture, and humanity itself. However, the moment right before birth is often a dangerous and complicated one. Our world today has reached a critical turning point. The passage into a better and brighter time will demand individuals and organizations that possess a force of creativity powerful enough to challenge the status quo, disrupt the marketplace, and transform society.

renaissance a movement or period of robust creative and intellectual activity that is associated with a rebirth of civilization.

generation a group of individuals born and living contemporaneously in a span of consecutive years, whose length approximates the span of a phase of life that is approximately twenty-two to thirty years.

RenGen explores the conditions that are giving rise to a generation on the verge of a second renaissance. Years into the knowledge economy, the context in which we live our daily lives is no longer a twilight zone of change. Who we are and what we care about is taking shape with an emerging set of imperatives, products, behaviors, and ambitions. After decades of hearing the mantra that life is all about change—a daily flood of circumstances impossible to navigate—it seems risky to be definitive about the larger patterns that are emerging. However, after spending two years researching our situation, I am convinced that we need to prepare ourselves for the possibility that we are poised to become a renaissance generation, a RenGen.

Comparing the flowering of the European Renaissance with the one emerging today reveals one essential difference: the speed of time. It took Western civilization from 1300 to 1500 to reach the point of "high Renaissance," the pinnacle of the age. Our renaissance is gearing up faster and will likely be shorter, lasting perhaps fewer than thirty years, a length of time experts agree to be "a generation."

In 1970, Alvin Toffler established a genre of futurist nonfiction with his seminal book, *Future Shock*. What followed was a welter of doomsday discourse. Today, many of us need no further convincing that the only given in life is an endless storm of change. As we search for effective strategies to make our way in a fractured, warp-speed world, this book makes one truth clear: we are sloughing off the old skin that defined us as unenlightened people and becoming a society preparing for a second renaissance. The evidence of it surrounds us, but most telling is the presence of the five preconditions that prepare a civilization for a renaissance.

Before sitting down to write this book, I had to group findings to see the patterns. I wanted to plot the process that leads up to a transformation as profound as a renaissance. But the differences between two civilizations separated by eight centuries are so great, that I focused on the catalytic conditions that share certain similarities, instead. These five conditions are described in the following sections: Death Comes First; The Rise of Beautiful Mind; The Collaborative Context; Catalytic People; and A Facilitating Medium.

Death Comes First

The origins of the first great renaissance were steeped in conflict and waste. At the dawn of the fourteenth century, Rome, having suffered one of many devastating fires, was in ruins. A long line of emperors had replaced the Republic, ruling with utter disregard for the collective will of the people. The economy was in shambles. In 1330, the plague swept across Europe. The chaos of war, economic degradation, large-scale death by a mysterious infection, and political corruption were forces that triggered a process of transformation catalyzed by an equally powerful force: the human imperative to invent ways to survive.

The Rise of Beautiful Mind

Original ideas come from someplace. Scientists who have researched the phenomena have found that the creative process involves the firing of neurons in search of something—usually a solution. Ideas begin with a hunt through our memory to reference something we already understand. We search our minds for a Potential Inspiration for New Ground (PING).

Consider the following example drawn from recent brain research. If I put in front of you an object that you have never seen before, you will search the storehouse of knowledge contained in your memory. "Where else have I seen something like this?" you ask yourself. If you can't find an answer you will keep PINGing. You may even begin to invent a meaning for the unexpected, or fuse an unknown object with things you are already familiar with for new inspiration. You are creating meaning to either relieve the uncomfortable dissonance, or you may simply be inspired by the unexpected, and this will trigger other iterations you can apply to a current problem. This is how we generate new ideas. The richer the storehouse of images and memory we have to PING against, the more combinations of answers and solutions we can conjure.

The beautiful mind is the gestalt of the RenGen. In the ideal state of a renaissance, culture operates at a heightened level of mental capacity. Hence, knowledge and information are powerful currency. As a society is presented with unprecedented problems it can no longer ignore, people begin searching for solutions. Those who have built large storehouses of information and show a facility for PINGing will be highly valuable.

The Collaborative Context

A renaissance is panoramic—it is an interlude of heightened context—not just a well-decorated setting where things happen.

Instead, the context is itself an organizing system from which social customs and meaning radiate. The rule of a renaissance is that context is important—in particular because it allows collaboration to occur. Collaboration is the way work gets done for the RenGen. Our conventional idea about creativity is that it is the domain of the artist. And when we think of artists we typically think of rugged individualists like Jackson Pollock, working away alone for hours in his studio. In truth, the Renaissance master Michelangelo assembled a large team of specialists to paint the Sistine Chapel. The very scale of the work undertaken—not to mention the amount of experimentation necessary—demanded the collective talents of many.

Our belief that creativity is the domain of artists also turns out to be a myth. There are many types of people who populate the creative context, such as master patrons, planners, expressives, auteurs, to name a few, and the more diverse the skill base, the more innovative the results.

Catalytic People

I traveled across the United States and parts of Europe in search of insights for this book. As with any journey, after awhile, the trees in the forest all look the same. People stand out, though. So, too, for the RenGen. There are specific personality types who animate the renaissance context, and I will take you back and forth across time periods so you can meet the personalities that drive a period of rebirth. Some of these people boldly lead the way, while others are like catalytic enzymes that cultivate the flourish to come.

A Facilitating Medium

A renaissance must have a facilitating medium that carries the flow of ideas and information. It is meaningless to attain knowledge if you then lack the means to apply and disseminate it. It is meaningless to receive inspiration without a means to express it. The facilitating medium serves both needs. The Roman Empire left behind an important gift to Western civilization: a vast network of roads that stretched across borders from Northern England to Mesopotamia, thereby connecting people to a larger world. Today, we have the Internet, which has had a gale-force impact on our culture.

Social Indicators Point to Rebirth

While the preconditions prepare the soil for a renaissance, social trends are proof that seeds are taking root. Next, we will address the evidence of that. Keep in mind that the following trends have been germinating over time and they are springing from grassroots activity—an indication that they'll have more staying power than fads that are typically driven from the top down.

The will to be reborn

This desire to "make me new again" drives everything from Botox to evangelism. For many, the imagined life encountered in all creative expression is a platform for what psychologist Abraham Maslow called "peak experiences" in which people discover new aspects of their potential only dreamed of before. The people we studied described being open to more possibilities and feeling rejuvenated or reborn when they created or experienced art, for example. Still others described the thrill of creating practical inventions to address social or mechanical challenges. The Italian renaissance was marked by the same fervor for new ideas and explorations that led to scientific discoveries, not to mention masterworks of art that now symbolize Western civilization.

Polarization and fusion

Renaissance people lived in an insecure world of religious factionalism, war, surprise attacks, and assassinations. You only need to skim the headlines to see that we too are experiencing the above. Given the multiplicity of threats that swarm around us, the typical person must strive to make sense of their world in order to function. There is also the overwhelming number of choices to make every day that add complexity. Hence, people create shortcuts by fusing disparate ideas into a single thing they can hold in their imaginations. Whether it be the fusion of science and art or mysticism and organized religion, renaissance people are adept at fusion. What cannot be fused may be polarized onto the margins.

The exaltation of roots

Scholars agree that one of the defining aspects of a renaissance is the fascination with the iconography and traditions of the past. A renaissance is not to be confused with a revolution; a renaissance builds on the bedrock of what came before. So, too, in our common culture is a palpable need to embrace aspects of our beliefs and customs that give us substance. Take, for example, the outpouring of emotion that followed the death of Pope John Paul II, who was laid to rest in St. Peter's Basilica, one of the most notable structures of the High Renaissance. Ardent and lapsed

Catholics alike followed the story, which was front-page news in most cities, as did people of many faiths around the world, in part because the papacy is a direct link to traditional roots.

Emphasis on visual and aural representation of ideas and information

Symbols, costumes, statues, icons, logos, and pictures become the predominant form of expression. They are a language. As the exchange of ideas happens more fluidly in a renaissance, and the geographies expand to reach a broader swath of people in distant lands, it is essential for communication to move from the specific to the universal to be understood. Written and spoken languages are specific, while visuals are universal. As the Renaissance swept across Europe, ideas could be represented in art, architecture, and everyday designs for clothing and household goods.

A respect for learning

A renaissance brings about a heightened appreciation for education. This is more about the aggressive exchange of ideas than the specious type of "seat learning" many of us grew up with. Knowledge becomes more accessible to the common man, and authoritarian experts are replaced by all forms of apprenticeship and collaborative exchanges among everyday people. The Renaissance saw the rise of home tutors. These were scholars and writers hired by the rising merchant class and nobles alike to teach the children in their households the lessons of the ancient Greeks, as well as basic literacy skills. Today, there is an increased emphasis on learning; whether it is facilitated by the Internet or delivered conventionally, learning is a priority. So much so that we call ourselves the "knowledge" society and managers in organizations are shifting their approach to deal with the new "knowledge worker."

Rise of the second cities

Renaissance periods take root in urban settings where the context is richest. Energy and resources are focused on an intensive interchange of ideas. Innovation can occur as a matter of daily life. Often—because death must come before rebirth—there is a dying off of the older cities or an exodus of talent, and new loci for creativity rise up.

Elevation of human potential

Some form of humanism is present within the context of a rebirth. Enlightenment and understanding are the business of everyone, not just the elites. It is up to the individual person to attain enlightenment, but each is fundamentally capable. The Renaissance was transformed spiritually and intellectually by humanism, which in a nutshell was a spirit of inquiry that held confidence in the ability of human beings to determine for themselves truth from falsehood. Today, in the United States, we have a well-developed sense of self-reliance. We believe in our ability to take action to improve our communities, schools, physical well-being, and emotional states. Step into any bookstore today and you will see an entire canon of self-help texts lining the walls.

A New Order

The confluence of these factors, made more complex by the number of choices we face each day from toothpaste to mortgages, calls out for a new order. How else will we keep it all straight? Unlike the linear, progressive ways of planning and executing new projects that came before, the RenGen is finding a new approach for managing complexity: the collage. Collage is the defining art form of the twenty-first century. The more people we interviewed, the more culture we observed, the more it became clear that collage is a metaphor for the RenGen. It captures the essence of the RenGen aesthetic. Collage is unpretentious, collaborative, interdisciplinary, recyclable, and flexible enough to be cocreated. And it is even a way of seeing how existing elements can fit with new ones to form unique things. Later in the book we will explore "collage theory" as a process for arriving at new solutions.

As you read this book, please keep one thing in mind: our worldwide situation holds tremendous potential. In a world poisoned by a century of progress at any price, it is easy to look around and believe we are in a freefall—socially, culturally, economically, and environmentally. But civilizations have cycles. This phase of the cycle has been trailing downward for some time. We are becoming aware that the environment and our survival in it are interconnected in perilous ways. We are becoming aware that the ideology and misplaced foreign policy of one country can fuel factionalism and terrorism in another. We are becoming aware that world financial markets are linked and interdependent in ways they never have been before. This is a point of crisis. A crisis that exists because people fear what will happen next. The values people once held dear, whether those are religious or civic values, gave them hope. Values of efficiency and profitability have yet to offer reasonable replacements. We are now witnessing the massing of culture, one based on new ideals seeking vigorous expression.

It is time to ask ourselves: What we should expect?

This book points the way to what lies beyond fear: a shift toward enlightenment that is dramatically changing the society in which we live and work. I am aiming here to help people who are now a part of the knowledge economy to recognize and understand the sea change that is occurring in their cities, their communities, and the markets they serve. In understanding the RenGen—as a segment of the population and as a cultural phenomenon—individuals and organizations can commit their talents, products, and services more profitably and purposefully to a society on the brink of a rebirth.

CHAPTER TWO

Seeds of Change— How a Renaissance Begins

When most people think of the Renaissance, they think of it as a time of accelerated creativity when several masters produced great works of art—works of art that are now the visual symbols that define Western civilization. In truth, that period when art and ideas blossomed across Europe occurred in the early fifteenth century, which is considered the High Renaissance. To understand how a phenomenon as potent as a renaissance occurs, it's helpful to understand what leads up to it. This means we need to go back a century earlier. Because scholars agree that Italy led the Renaissance, it's worth taking the journey back to fourteenth-century Rome, which at that time was a city hovering between life and death.

In 1300, the Florentine writer Fillipo Villani traveled to Rome on a quest to "behold the great and ancient things." Here is what he found: the Coliseum stood in partial ruin, its inner ring overgrown with weeds. Sheep grazed on the Palatine Hill, where the residences of the great emperors once stood. Everything that met Villani's gaze told him Rome was dying. It is not overstating the matter to see the impact of Rome's fall as the end of the world, or at least the end of the world as people knew it. Rome was once the center of everything—a worldview shared by many in Europe, none more than the Romans themselves.

Visit Rome today and you can still find a spot at the base of the Capitoline Hill in the Roman Forum where senators once stood and delivered great oratory. If you look closely you can make out the Latin phrase chiseled into the stone floor: *umbilicus mundi*, which translates into "belly button of the world." But by the time Villani made his way there in 1300, "Rome was not a center of commerce or industry, it was not even the ecclesiastical center of Europe; it was the home of symbolic vestiges; haunted by the recollection of greatness far beyond that of any modern city," writes George Holmes, author of *Florence, Rome and the Origins of the Renaissance*. Romans saw reminders of their fall everywhere, and it is probably fair to say that the psychological toll was devastating.

If the symbolic death of Rome were not traumatic enough, the arrival of the Black Death in 1340 surely was. The rat-flea virus that swept the bubonic plague across Asia and Europe was an equal-opportunity killer. In its already declining state, Rome was emptied. Marchione di Coppo Stefani, describes the grisly effects of the plague:

Neither physicians nor medicines were effective. Whether because these illnesses were previously unknown or because physicians had not previously studied them, there seemed to be no cure. There was such a fear that no one seemed to know what to do. When it took hold in a house it often happened that no one remained who had not died. And it was not just that men and women died, even sentient animals died. Dogs, cats, chickens, oxen, donkeys, sheep showed the same symptoms and died of the same disease. And almost none, or very few, who showed these symptoms, were cured. . . . It was such a frightful thing that when it got into a house, as was said, no one remained. Frightened people abandoned the house and fled to another.

It is important to understand that no matter how grim a death a society experiences, the cultural ashes that come from such a fall fertilize its soil for new growth.

I grew up in the Midwest, where a person is never too far away from farm life. In the summers of my childhood, my family escaped industrial Detroit for the cool, open air of northern Michigan. One holiday, we took a detour. Our lumbering Oldsmobile clicked past rows of blue-green cornfields occasionally interrupted by gnarled clumps of soybean plants. I'd rest my arms on the open window and tilt my face out into the breeze where I could take in the loamy smell of soil and corn plants. By and by, we passed a farmer driving a tractor across the soybean field. It looked to me as if the machine was chopping up the plants—destroying them. I asked my father about it, who explained that this was "plowing under," which is how farmers prepare the soil for a good harvest. That is the law of a RenGen. Death comes first.

Death of Character

The Renaissance writer Leonardo Bruni laments a different kind of loss—the death of what he called "the Roman character." Bruni was a Florentine who observed that the combination of imperial crime and the elevation of violence encouraged by emperors like

the notoriously self-indulgent Nero had debased the very character of the Roman people. That loss of character, Bruni argued, was
a side effect of the citizen's loss of liberty under Nero's regime. In
other words, it was not political corruption itself that tumbled the
Empire, it was the withering away of the character of the Roman
people who eventually came to accept such corruption and violence as something out of their control; under the Republic, by
contrast, they had enjoyed some measure of self-determination.

What was the Roman character, you might wonder? If you
are like most people, you picture the Romans of Nero's time as
overfed and oversexed. But the period of the Republic was a different matter. Under the rule of the Senate, a hearty economy
flourished, buttressed by a sophisticated banking system, and the
people were governed by a representative civic authority. Some
of Rome's most impressive structures were built in this phase,
all facilitated by Rome's unmatched military might. On this
point, scholars agree that impressive progress was made when
the Roman Senate governed. "To understand the difference in
results between self-determination encouraged by the Republic
versus the absolute power of the emperors, we should weigh how
Rome grew but little under the kings, but acquired the Empire
over the world within a short period of time under the senate,"
comments historian Cino Rinuccini. The Republic allowed for
the free flow of ideas because it allowed greater personal liberty.
This sense of freedom is described often in the writings of Bruni
and his contemporaries as a cherished right that future Italian
cities, most especially Florence, would seek to emulate. Much
later, Machiavelli would warn leaders in his enduring book, *The
Prince*, that "men do not accept less liberty," once they have tasted
it—implying that it cannot be ripped from them, only gradually

worn away. The traits of ambition and ingenuity were aspects of the "Roman character" that built Rome and nourished it into an Empire. To put it another way, when despotic rule replaced the Republic, people slowly quit striving for a certain way of life.

Life Cycles of Civilization

Others have examined the cycle of death and life of civilizations. In 1941, Pitirim Sorokin published his influential book, *The Crisis of Our Age.* Sorokin was a native of Touria, Russia. His perspective on the life cycle of cultures may have been informed by his own experiences with the tumultuous rise of the Bolshevik party and by his own rise and fall as a young scholar in Russia—from which he was banished in 1922. He fled to the United States, where he eventually joined the faculty at Harvard to create the university's first department of sociology.

Sorokin was fascinated by what he considered the unavoidable decline of great societies. In his three volumes of research, Sorokin theorized that the life cycle of civilizations follows a "double process" of decline and rebirth, which happen in slow, concentric loops. Sorokin and, later, Mihaly Csikszentmihalyi, the renowned expert on the "flow of creativity" who was influenced by Sorokin's work, find agreement in the idea that the interlude between life and death cycles of a civilization can stimulate a flowering or rebirth as the culture creatively fuses where it's been with where it may be headed. As the civilization dies, it throws off seeds for the next cycle, which is often a more expressive one as society is striving to make new meaning out of what has preceded it and what is now emerging.

How we assign meaning to our experience defines the culture. These cultural mind-sets are somewhat ordered, and follow rhythmic cycles, Sorokin concludes. We are now in a sensate cycle that is overripe and ready to die. A sensate civilization is based on satisfaction of senses—food, material comfort, and utilitarian purposes. In a sensate society, people use material objects to convey meaning. The society is less concerned with art and philosophy to communicate meaning. The sensate culture strives for ease of living and efficiency. Roman civilization was sensate.

The cycle that follows the sensate is more ideological; it is based on transcendence from material concerns. Sorokin explains "People turn their attention to religion or ideology and view their challenges in terms of . . . reaching inner clarity and conviction." Ideas eclipse the importance of things.

The most important thing to understand about Sorokin's theory of the life cycles of civilizations is that large-scale change is *built in*—as opposed to being externally induced. The calamities that befall a society will certainly hasten its fall, but the decline is a predetermined natural force just like the waxing and waning of the moon, but on a much grander scale. This theory places the power of the human mind at its center. The mind creates meaning from the phenomena that come with change. And if the mind-set becomes a collective force—that is, it is shared by a large enough mass of people—a new culture is formed. Once the "cultural mentality" emerges, it propels new ideas of what is significant and what is no longer relevant.

Sorokin warned that the declining culture must be careful to avoid undue stress in its weakened state; otherwise, it would thwart the next cycle. He went so far as to anticipate that, if the forces of the decaying order were to start a new world war, then, "dissipating their remaining energy, these forces can end or greatly impede the creative progress of mankind. If this apocalyptic catastrophe can be avoided, then the emerging creative forces will usher humanity into a new magnificent era of its history." In other words, if the conditions do not favor a renaissance, it is also possible for the synthesis between the two cycles to fail. Like the hand-off between trapeze artists, it is possible to fall into something resembling the Dark Ages. However, my research into what is occurring presently gives me reason to be optimistic.

The Rise of the Second City

Contributing to the decay of the Empire and its accomplishments was a flight of "gifted minds" from Rome, as Bruni describes it. Once original ideas ceased, and the places people shared those ideas lay vacant, the civilization reached a turning point. Fillipo Villani surmises as much: "Considering that our city of Florence, the daughter and creature of Rome, was rising, and had great things before her, whilst Rome was declining, it seemed to me fitting to collect in this volume and in the year 1300, having returned from Rome, I began to write this book." Villani decided to chronicle the decline of Rome and the rise of Florence. In so doing, he left a record of the emergence of the Italian renaissance.

It would be a mistake to think that Florence was impervious to broader crises such as the plague. It was hit hard, as well. But by then the Roman brain drain was well underway and many of the artists, scientists, and thinkers of the time were living in

Florence. It is impossible to say exactly how this elite population in particular was affected by the plague, but by the time it
had passed, Florence took up the mantle as the second city—the
younger sibling that was coming into its own. These Florentines,
descendents of those free Romans of the Republican era, shuf-
fled off their medieval hull and emerged as a vibrant citystate,
one that set the example for other citystates in the regions of
Umbria and Tuscany based on a commitment to civic freedom
and humanism. Florence also had the benefit of the wealthy
Medici family, who aggressively supported festivals, public art,
and scholarship to make Florence an exciting place to live and
work. The effect was to entice people already inclined to break
away from conventions to experiment with novelty beyond what
would be likely in a more provincial setting.

A Facilitating Medium

For many centuries, the Roman Empire rested on the broad
shoulders of its infantry. Regardless of whether the Senate or
Caesar ruled, progress depended upon these carefully recruited,
highly trained, and well-led soldiers. As Nigel Sitwell writes in
his book *Roman Roads of Europe*: "It was these legionnaires
who ultimately ensured efficient, uniform administrative standards, gigantic ambitious building projects, mesmeric but suc-
cinct Forum oratory, a guaranteed peace and real certainty of its
continuation for the majority, and an extremely, luxurious and
decadent lifestyle for the few." Such military effectiveness was
facilitated by the roads the soldiers built to transport large military machinery, legions of troops, and supplies.

Eventually, the vast network of roads led to other efficiencies. For instance, the Roman government could rule their territories and collect taxes, as Sitwell writes, "with an army of 180,000 legionnaires, plus auxiliaries—a figure markedly out of proportion to the total population of 55 million."

What mattered most for the rise of the Renaissance is that its roads became a network for communicating. Similar to the Pony Express many of us remember from our American history instruction, this organization of couriers spanned the entire Empire with post houses and inns along major routes. Post houses, where horses could be switched, were plotted every ten to fifteen miles, and inns gave tavern-like accommodation similar to a modern roadhouse. Early in the days of the Empire, private citizens could use the roads by seeking a permit. Although the rule was strictly enforced, the roads still facilitated the controlled exchange of information and ideas across the Empire. Evidence is found in letters between Trajan (emperor from AD 98–117) and the historian Pliny, who wrote to seek permission to use an outdated permit to deliver some dispatches. Sitwell writes: "The emperor's response was short and curt, he stated: 'It is my invariable rule to have fresh permits sent to each province before the dates are required'."

As the Empire declined, use of the roads by civilians was common. Roman roads were so designed and constructed that little repair was required, except on the wooden bridges. Many were still in perfect working order centuries after their construction. Entire towns grew up along the routes, and the roads became a medium for communicating the aggressive intellectual expression that would pour forth with the rise of the Renaissance.

While the Romans roads spurred on the Renaissance of old, a similar phenomenon is seen with the Internet of today, with the vast computer network creating an open forum of idea development and exchange. Yet as the Roman roads were finite, restricted by tangible barriers such as available land, the Internet has the potential to continue to expand unfettered.

As part of a new emerging renaissance, we should prepare ourselves for the possibility that our most innovative days are ahead of us. Although, like the Romans, we have experienced a difficult period of decline that might otherwise have the power to crush us, that is not going to happen. In fact, the conditions are in place for a very different and dynamic outcome, facilitated by technology, catalyzed by human talent, and inspired by a new mind-set. This we will discuss in the next chapter.

CHAPTER THREE

The Beautiful Mind

What separates one era from another is usually a discovery or event that fundamentally alters the way people understand their world. Simply put, it changes their mind-set: The world is flat, the world is round; what goes up must come down; God made the world, man is the product of evolution and natural selection—and so it goes. The label *RenGen* is less about a specific age group and more about a particular mind-set. A change in mind-set is a reorganization of meaning, and the way we derive meaning from life determines the psychic fabric of the common culture.

By the 1300s, people began to see the power of man in his environment. Scholars would later term this the rise of "humanism," and it reordered man's place in the world. A person could comprehend and commune directly with God, without a designated go-between such as a priest. Because man could have a sacred relationship with his God, he could begin to express a personal vision for what had been unknowable and invisible. This was elevating. Humanism brought with it a new sense of the value of life, along with a new appreciation of each person's ability to contribute to the world.

How powerful was the shift in mind-set? Consider what followed: Gutenberg's printing of the Bible in the 1440s and the Protestant Reformation begun by Martin Luther in 1517. Such events had many more implications for the arts and sciences—some of which we'll explore as we toggle back and forth between past and present.

A Shift in Mind-set

Cognitive dynamics, or how we build knowledge, is more easily understood in a context—that cosmos of things, images, and customs that form a person's reality. In his book *Cities of God*, historian Augustine Thompson makes the case for the importance of considering the Renaissance man in relation to his religion. Thompson meticulously traces the influence of the Church on the daily lives of people—what they saw, heard, talked about, touched—threads that, woven together, formed a lifestyle encompassing religion, civic affairs, and family ties. Drawing from a staggering wealth of evidence gathered from ecclesiastical statutes, tithe lists, memoirs of saints, street maps, art and architecture, Thompson paints a sacred geography that is the context for daily life in the early 1300s, the period preceding the full flowering of the Renaissance. According to Thompson: "This was an urban environment tightly packed with religious expressions everywhere: cathedrals, baptisteries, civic palazzos dedicated to patron saints, statuary, processions, costumes, candle offerings and bell ringing." In the world Thompson depicts, God and the natural world, as well as man's place in it, are intertwined, touchable, and seeable—and therefore knowable.

It would be a mistake to think the humanistic mind-set was revolutionary. A renaissance was not a revolution. The new outlook grew up alongside more ancient traditions that were realized in the buildings and art that were daily fixtures in people's lives. This perspective brought with it a secularization of knowledge that made it possible for many more people to lend their voices to the discussion. People felt free to contribute intellectually, spiritually, and creatively to their society. They acquired and displayed art, embroidered historical scenes into their clothing, and marched in liturgical parades carrying statues and paintings—all of which contributed to stimulating visual culture.

Humanism also altered the labor market. Scholars found regular employment translating ancient texts and embellished passages where meaning was unclear to create new genres that were more accessible. What's important to understand is that the shift in mind-set was catalytic: Humanism produced a sort of psychic energy that fueled the rise of the first RenGen. As it turned out, that fuel was also combustible. Combined with the right ingredients it would ignite a rebirth.

The Transcendental Imagination

The question of how we derive meaning from life is a persistent theme among researchers and experts on creativity. Because a renaissance is associated with a great outpouring of creativity, it helps us to consider how people derive meaning in a creative environment. Robert Nozick, the late Harvard professor of philosophy, believed that meaning could only begin to be understood in relation to something that is already meaningful. In other words, our imaginations move from the concrete to the abstract, not the other way around. In his book, *Philosophical Explanations*, Nozick writes: "About any given thing, however wide, it seems we can stand back and ask what its meaning is. To find meaning for it, we seem driven to find a link with yet another thing beyond its boundaries . . . something which is unlimited." What Nozick describes is transcendence: the ability to move from the concrete to the abstract and then beyond into a greater unknown.

This idea of transcendence carries with it the possibility of moving beyond our limitations into something more expansive. The idea that we can transcend the unknowable to create meaning has stimulated scholarship for several centuries.

Eighteenth-century German philosopher Immanuel Kant argued that there are two kinds of knowledge: ordinary knowledge, which is knowledge of objects; and transcendental knowledge, which is how we experience those objects in ways that lie beyond what our intellects can know. In the thirteenth century, the theologian Thomas Aquinas described the movement from the known to the imaginary as a creative activity, in which "the imagination forms for itself an image of something absent, or something never seen." More recently, the pioneering psychologist Abraham Maslow's famous "hierarchy of needs" identifies the need to understand the self and aesthetic appreciation as steps toward a transcendent state. There is a connection between the need to see "beyond" what is obvious, to glimpse at something never seen, and the creative imagination. Because a renaissance represents a period of heightened creativity, let's take a look at how the mind works in this way.

PING—Or the Anatomy of an Idea

Original ideas come from someplace. Scientists have studied the changes that take place in brain function when subjects are presented with something unexpected. Although there are numerous variations, perception usually follows this path: The eye sees something and the brain poses questions; in a snap, neurons fire in search of reference points and hone in on an answer. You see an object and your brain answers "chair" . . . it is a type of chair. But what if I put an object in front of you that you have never seen before? In that case, you will search your memory and ask it: "Where have I seen something like this?" No answer. You will keep searching your brain, checking the nooks and crannies of your cortex. All the while you are rapidly forming an assessment of whether this thing could harm you. Unsure, you may begin to invent a way of classifying and understanding the object. You might refine it by fusing it with a known object, thus inventing something original. This is how we generate new ideas. We search for what I term **p**otential **i**nspiration for **n**ew **g**round—or PING The richer our storehouse of images and knowledge we have to PING against, the more combinations of answers and solutions we can conjure.

Each of us has two organizing repositories of information: the information in our genetic code and the information stored in our brains. We are concerned here with the latter. In the 1940s, John von Neumann, a mathematician and nuclear physicist, made important contributions to understanding the processes of the brain in storing and accessing information. A member of the Manhattan Project that developed the technology for the atomic bomb, von Neumann is considered to have been an early pioneer of artificial intelligence. His work on the modern digital

computer led him to wonder how humans store and access information—ostensibly so he could determine whether a similar
architecture could be automated, using what he called "cellular
automata," his term for artificial intelligence.

In his book, *The Computer and the Brain*, von Neumann
describes what occurs in our brains when we encounter complex
problems: essentially, a messaging system carries a single train of
pulses across a bundle of fibers, each of which transmits pulses.
Without having the advanced technology of today at his disposal,
von Neumann could only theorize that certain pulse frequencies
were associated with the brain's search through its storehouse
when it sought to solve a complex new problem. Acknowledg-
ing his own limitations, von Neumann conceded that a new,
essentially logical theory would need to be created to explain
this phenomenon.

Von Neumann's early theory of the brain emitting high-fre-
quency pulsations as it probes for solutions is consistent with
the notion of PING. And von Neumann's call for a new theory
was answered: Subsequent research on the brain has revealed
that the human brain fires possibilities, images, and information
across its geography, thus triggering cognitive and sensory activity that forms original solutions.

In 2005, in a laboratory in Sydney, Australia, three scientists
used an EEG to measure what happens to brain activity in 100
healthy adults when certain aspects of their environment are
changed. Drs. Donald Rowe, Peter Robinson, and Christopher
Rennie specifically tracked how the brain fires when it detects
unexpected stimuli. They were also interested in measuring
thresholds of tolerance for stimulation. When, for instance, do
stimuli go from being acceptably unusual to threateningly weird?

Subjects were asked to close and then open their eyes. Each time, they were presented with new stimuli. The researchers discovered that firing rates increase across the entire mass of the brain when unexpected objects are encountered, as opposed to localized firing when people encounter familiar objects or experiences.

Perhaps more significant, they found that the entire brain gets stronger as a result of the activity; it develops "synaptic strength" to fire faster and endure stimulation for longer periods. Finally, there is a spin-off effect in the brain that opens more ion channels for receiving information and decreases membrane resistance to more input. This is scientific evidence of what might commonly be construed as open-mindedness—an important factor in a renaissance mind-set.

Willemien Otten, a contemporary German scholar who has devoted her career to the relationship between medieval religion and civic life, describes the Renaissance as an "opening up." In her words, "ordinary people engaged in the professions and crafts, and they created and enjoyed works of art." This sense of the "opening up" of the mind is what von Neumann suspected, and what the Australian researchers measured.

Dissolving the Barriers that Constrict Flow

The democratization of knowledge we share today has gale-force impact, just as humanism had during the first Renaissance. Much has been written about the decline of the "noted expert" on everything from film criticism to advice on improving your sex life. In fact, in the world of blogging, *everyone*'s a critic.

According to Pew Internet and American Life, by 2004, there were already between 2.4 million and 2.9 million active blogs, and 44% of U.S. Internet users created and contributed content for the Web. Intellectual life in America traditionally has been the discrete business of academics and publishing houses. Academics were granted the time and encouragement to think and write, along with access to research facilities and major library collections to assist them. Publishers have traditionally worked in their own inner circle, and for those who publish in the popular media, there is support available for intellectual contributions from their colleagues, who review and applaud their work.

But that is changing. One of the pioneers of that change is John Brockman, a larger-than-life author, intellectual impresario, and editor of books including *What We Believe but Cannot Prove: Today's Leading Thinkers on Science in the Age of Certainty.* Brockman's career spans science, technology, and journalism; currently, he runs his own agency representing authors. He has been exalted as a first-rate intellect and vilified as a hustler promoting scientists with commercially powerful ideas. Brockman believes there is a third culture, one that stands outside academia and traditional publishing. Brockman has built an online "salon" called The Edge to facilitate its rise. Here's how he expressed the mission on his Web site *(www.edge.org)* in March 2006: "Throughout history, intellectual life has been marked by the fact that only a small number of people have done the serious thinking for everybody else. What we are witnessing is a passing of the torch from one group of thinkers, the traditional literary intellectuals, to a new group, the intellectuals of the emerging third culture."

Brockman's notion of a third culture is really about an opening up, a democratization of information and thought. In essence, he is describing the RenGen mind-set. The market Brockman is tapping into stems from a civilization driven, perhaps by instinct, to gain access to challenging ideas that force us to build our storehouse of knowledge so that we can make new meaning.

Big Threats, Big Ideas

So, what situation might have the magnitude to put society into PING mode? What unseen, unknowable threat might endanger our survival? As Meryl Streep's character in the 2004 remake of *The Manchurian Candidate* tells her son the political candidate, the American people sense the threat, they aren't sure when it will come or where it will come from, but it is out there, waiting to destroy us.

As we teeter on the verge of a second renaissance, the level of threat in our daily environment is increasing. While this threat may come from overhead, delivered by hijacked aircraft or nuclear attack, research is starting to suggest that it is more likely to shower down gently in the form of acid rain from an environment that is seriously compromised.

During the summer of 2006 while I was writing this chapter, *Vanity Fair* and *People* magazines both devoted their front covers to the environment, granting star status to workaday advocates alongside movie stars like Bette Midler and George Clooney. *The New Yorker* reflected on the gut punch that Al Gore's road show and movie *An Inconvenient Truth* delivers on the environment. Consider this from Gore's published essay in *Vanity Fair*: "Global warming, together with the cutting and burning of forests and the destruction of critical habitats, is causing the loss of living species at a rate comparable to that of the extinction of dinosaurs 65 million years ago. . . All of this, incredibly, could be set in motion in the lifetime of the children already living. . . . (S)cientific experts are now telling us that without dramatic changes, we are in grave danger of crossing a point of no return within the next 10 years!" Previously an invisible threat, the compromised environment has been linked with the following events, which people around the world can see for themselves on television and the Internet:

- Melting polar ice caps
- Devastating floods
- Rising sea levels that subsume shorelines
- Blasts of warm air that form fronts like the one that powered Hurricane Katrina

In that same month that I was writing this book, the *New York Times* published an article on the front page of its Sunday edition, "Pollution from Chinese Coal Cast Shadow Around Globe." The article spoke to the precarious environmental situation that is being created by China's rapid industrialization: "The increase in global warming gases from China's coal use will probably exceed that of all industrialized countries combined over the next 25 years . . ." The article continues: "To make matters worse, India is right behind China in stepping up its construction of coal-fired power plants—and has a population expected to outstrip China's by 2030."

Soon after, *NBC Nightly News* ran a story warning holiday vacationers that more than one-quarter of the nation's beaches were considered unsafe due to pollution run-off and bacterial loads in the water.

Intrigued by this news, I decided to try a little experiment. With the help of Betty Laliberte, the reference librarian at my local public library, I tracked the growth of "ecophobia," a term coined by David Sobel, a science teacher and author, which means fear of ecological problems such as oil spills, rainforest destruction, acid rain, and the ozone hole.

While searching media databases, Betty and I discovered a trend. In Salt Lake City, for instance, the number of news stories on "global warming" grew from only three mentions in 1990 to 74 in 2005. The trend held true from Cincinnati to Santa Fe. Houston was the only exception. With little effort, we gathered a sizable stack of material on global warming culled from daily newspapers. It is impossible to refute the gradual escalation of information confronting the average person. The RenGen now perceives a serious threat to its survival. It may or may not turn out to be as sweeping as the plague, but for now there is considerable evidence that it is forceful enough to urge society into the second renaissance.

The Fit Brain Is Its Own Reward

Survival, however, is not the only motivation for problem-solving. As it turns out, all of this mental activity has its own rewards: it is pleasurable and good for us. At Rush Medical Center in Chicago, researchers studied groups of elderly individuals with a variety of symptoms that might lead to the onset of Alzheimer's disease. Working from a baseline of brain function, subjects were studied over a period of five years. Those who engaged in activities that were mentally stimulating—participating in book clubs, doing crossword puzzles, studying history, writing poetry, taking how-to classes, and so on—were 47 percent less likely to develop Alzheimer's than subjects who had not participated in such activities. The researchers concluded that the fit brain is more resilient, can perceive and process more quickly, and has more working memory at its disposal.

I expect the rise of the RenGen to bring with it a fascination for the fit brain. People will begin to crave mental workouts as well as physical ones. The evidence for this is already emerging. Staffers at the New York Public Library, for instance, were surprised recently when the library's lecture series began selling out—and to a much younger audience than had previously attended. Paul Holdengraber, the library's director of public programs, explained it to a reporter at the *New York Times* this way: "It's not only sex that sells, but the life of the mind. When you come into contact with a great idea, it can change your life." If Sorokin is correct in his assessment that the declining "sensate" culture we are shedding had its obsessions with the body, then the coming "idealogical" civilization we are entering will balance that the sensate with an array of activities, objects, and situations aimed at stimulating the mind.

Like most things we crave, there is likely some anticipatory and unconscious reason for the craving. Athletes crave liquids to replace electrolytes drained through overexertion, for example. Taken together, all of this information compels us to look around and be alert to the changes that will come. Clearly, the RenGen will have fit minds, a changing mind-set, and an aesthetic sensibility to go with them, which we will explore next.

CHAPTER FOUR

The Creative Personality

Any discussion of a renaissance inevitably leads to an exploration of creativity. This book is concerned with the economic aspects of today's knowledge economy and the heightened interest in popular culture for creative self-expression; this makes the topic of creativity not just a point of interest, but an essential piece of the puzzle. Unlike the Italian renaissance, we live in an age when science can harness human functions, such as vision and language, to engineer software that can scan a face and interpret emotions. This type of technology heightens the potential for where creativity can take us as a civilization.

The race is on to discover the definitive link between creativity and cognition. The term *cognition* comes from the Latin *cognito*, meaning "to think." Formidable interests have a stake in understanding how the creative mind works. Companies like Google™, IBM, and Microsoft® are sponsoring forums at which scientists share research in this fast-emerging field. Where is all this research headed? Well, if we can trace a path in the brain from the point at which a problem or opportunity is detected to the moment of discovery or solution, that path could be retraced. And if it can be retraced, it can be replicated. This is the basis of artificial intelligence (AI).

Scientists at the Center for Creativity and Cognition in Australia are conducting experiments that replicate PINGing by using digital interfaces designed to channel intuitive interaction between humans and computers. This is one example of an emerging field of research focused on how the creative processes of the mind work—a field that incorporates a wide variety of scientific disciplines including psychology, biology, anthropology, sociology, education, robotics, and computer science. The sophistication demanded by this research has led to a collaboration of talented experts.

Stocking the Storehouse

At first, many people (especially those on Wall Street) considered it simply a curiosity when Google, with its vast financial resources, decided to digitize the holdings of five university libraries—collections that encompass all the intellectual resources of our civilization from the dawn of the written word. Imagine the wealth of material to PING against! While attending a conference in New York for the online advertising community, I stumbled across an inside look on Google's larger agenda for its library digitization project, a brand named Google Scholar. As I crossed the ballroom where a panel discussion had just wrapped up, I encountered John Battelle, author of the book, *The Search: How Google and Its Rivals Rewrote the Rules of Business and Transformed Our Culture*, which is an exploration of the financial and cultural importance of Google. I was attending the conference to gather information for a client; I never expected to learn the deeper purpose behind Google's aggressive digitization of the written word.

Battelle, is a tall, angular man who wears stylish eyeglasses and looks to be thirtyish. He punctuates his talk with a youthful bounce. I opened with a general question about Google Scholar and he started by telling me about Google's business model. But when I asked him why Google was bothering to digitize the collections of major libraries, he came to rest. He leaned back and assessed me, as if deciding whether to share his next thought. "It's not about serving up more sponsored links," he said. "It has nothing to do with the current profit center. It's all about AI." Like the techno-peasant that I am, I asked him what AI meant. In the manner of a helpful graduate assistant, he smiled politely and said, "Artificial intelligence." By engorging large university library collections into its massive algorithmic reservoir, Google apparently is building a super-brain capable of PINGing at high speeds against billions of pieces of premium data. Battelle pulled out a card and scribbled the name George Dyson on the back. "Check him out. He's blogged about it." With that, he stepped away, into a buzzing hive of technology journalists.

I did as he suggested and looked up George Dyson online. Scientist and cultural observer, Dyson is one of a new breed of philosophers who contribute their thoughts at the intersection of technology, science, and culture. This growing cadre of intellectuals is itself indicative of the RenGen, since it represents a clear democratization of knowledge. Some of these intellectuals are scientists, but most are not traditional scholars. Although they might hold professorships, they are public thinkers who engage broader questions facing mankind, and they feel free to connect their ideas to disciplines outside their academic domain, including art and poetry. Returning to my hunt to discover Google's long-range plans to develop artificial intelligence, I sought out Dyson—by Googling him, of course. In one of his blog entries, Dyson described his visit to Google's Silicon Valley headquarters this way:

> Despite the whimsical furniture and other toys, I felt I was entering a 14th-century cathedral—not in the 14th century but in the 12th century, while it was being built. Everyone was busy carving one stone here and another stone there, with some invisible architect getting everything to fit. The mood was playful, yet there was a palpable reverence in the air. "We are not scanning all those books to be read by people," explained one of my hosts after my talk. "We are scanning them to be read by an AI." (from "Turing's Cathedral," at *www.edge.org*, 10/24/05)

It is difficult to predict how artificial intelligence will change our world, since it has countless possible applications. Nicholas Negroponte, co-founder of MIT's storied Media Lab, pondered a world where "things think" and concluded that virtually all the appliances could be imbued with artificial intelligence. But the higher goal is to make artificial intelligence that can reason and is self-aware, a breakthrough that would thrust forward an already accelerated knowledge society.

Why People Are Creative

If you accept that the act of conceiving something completely original is a mix—part discovery, part referential, part visionary and part "ardor," as Tchaikovsky described it—then you can appreciate that the creative process is difficult to analyze. It is more than billions of pieces of data PINGing against each other at high speeds. Focusing on the mental properties of problem-solving alone will not give us full insight into the creative imagination. Mihaly Cskikszymhaly, author of *Creativity: Flow and the Psychology of Discovery and Invention,* argues that "creativity does not happen in people's heads" but in [the] interaction between a person's imagination and a social context. Although researchers are more willing to define creativity by what it is *not*, there have been distinctive evaluations of the people who are judged to be creative by their peers. When evaluations of these highly creative individuals are studied consistencies do emerge.

In the 1990s, John R. Hayes, a professor at Carnegie Mellon University in Pittsburgh, documented three decades of research on people who were identified as creative by their peers. Hayes was looking for human characteristics that could be associated with the creative process. He did a sweeping analysis of data from studies done on creative types; his research included scientists whose careers were marked with important breakthroughs, as well as architects and artists from a variety of disciplines.

Hayes wanted to see what kinds of people are creative, and what motivates them to create. He drew a line dividing people who showed creative productivity in realized works from those with "unexpressed potential." This distinction suggests the importance of social context, because Hayes paid attention only to creative acts resulting in work with some significance to the broader society, based on recognition or usefulness, and his ultimate test was that the work be completely original.

As it happened, what he didn't find turned out to be as important as what he did, because it gave clues to the facets of a highly creative personality. For instance, Hayes did not find that creative people are any smarter than their noncreative counterparts. Of the 504 physical and biological scientists selected for research productivity, no correlation was found between creativity and either I.Q. or school grades. Hayes considered a 1963 study of two samples of chemists and mathematicians who were matched in age, education, and experience. Among the first sample of people considered by peers to produce creative work, I.Q. played no role. They out-published the others at a rate of 8 to 1, but there was no difference between them in either I.Q. or school grades. What set them apart was an intrinsic motivation to create—that is, to produce original work and solve difficult problems.

While experts agree that it is difficult to measure the brain's creative function, researchers have been more successful in identifying personality traits in creative people. These traits can be grouped into five categories:

- Productivity
- Independence
- Drive for originality
- Flexibility
- Aspiration

Let's explore these traits more closely in the context of the RenGen.

Productivity

Creative people work hard. While their toil can span several years of silent effort before they emerge with a remarkable invention or work of art, they devote themselves, almost exclusively, to their work. Consider that Herbert Simon, a Nobel laureate in economics, logged about 100 hours per week for years doing the work on decision making in organizations for which he eventually won the prize. Hayes describes physicists and biologists who were considered creative:

> There is only one thing that seems to characterize the total group, and that is absorption in their work, over long years, and frequently to the exclusion of everything else. . . . This one thing alone is probably not of itself sufficient to account for the success enjoyed by these people, but it appears to be a sine qua non.

While there may be long gaps between periods of creative output, it would be a mistake to think that such a gap means the creator has taken a break or suffered a block. It is common for there to be long quiet periods during which intensive experimentation is going on. There is very wide agreement among researchers that preparation is one of the most important conditions of creativity. By *preparation*, I mean the effort of the creative person, often over long periods, to acquire a large enough reservoir of knowledge and skills to PING against, ultimately resulting in creativity. Hayes gives strong evidence that even the most talented composers and painters—e.g., Mozart and van Gogh—required years of preparation before they began to produce the work for which they are famous.

In Harold Schonberg's book, *The Lives of the Great Composers*, the author used biographical data to determine when each of the seventy-six composers first became seriously interested in music, determined by when they began piano lessons in earnest. He identified the notable works of each and the dates when they were composed. (A work was considered notable if there were at least five different recordings of it on the market.) From these data, he calculated how many years it took, from the onset of serious interest to the resulting creative product. Out of more than 500 works, only three were composed before year 10 of the composer's career, and those three were composed in years 8 and 9. Averaged over the group, the pattern of career productivity was an initial ten-year period of silence, a rapid increase in productivity from year 10 to year 25, a period of stable productivity from year 25 to about year 45 and then a gradual decline.

This business of working hard toward a masterwork is true across a variety of disciplines. A parallel study used biographical data on 131 painters to determine when each became seriously involved in painting. Notable works of these painters were defined as ones that appeared in one of the major published histories of art. The pattern of productivity for the painters was similar to that for the composers: There was an initial period of silence, which in the painters' case lasted about six years. This was followed by a rapid increase in productivity over the next six years, a period of stable productivity until about thirty-five years into career and then a period of declining productivity, no doubt attributable to age. A similar biographical study of renowned poets found that none of sixty-six poets in the cohort had written a notable poem until at least five years into their careers.

Together, these studies suggest that long periods of preparation are important for creative productivity even for the most talented of musicians, painters, and poets. There is significant early working, gathering of information, honing of skills, and relentless experimentation, followed by a return to research to explain what failed or succeeded and why. This general pattern supports the theory of PING, and its functioning in the creative process.

Independence

Creative people also have a strong drive for independence. They want to make their own decisions about how they use their time and talents. Hayes explains that, the creative scientist "... is not the type of person who waits for someone else to tell him what to do, but rather thinks things through and then takes action on his own with little regard to convention." Furthermore: "When seeking a position . . . the overwhelming choice for the creative scientists is the opportunity to do really creative research and to choose problems of interest to them."

The Westinghouse Science Talent Search offers a window into the inner-directed nature of the creative person. The contest was established in 1942 to identify young, remarkably creative science students. Today, the program is sponsored by Intel®, and uses similar criteria: high school students are chosen on the basis of self-initiated projects rather than written tests or grades. They receive very general guidelines and very little formal guidance, and their projects are evaluated by two scientists in the relevant field. The goal—currently of Intel, and of Westinghouse before it—is to identify young scientists driven to do original work. In the group of 2,400 students who have participated since the contest's inception, there are five Nobel Prize winners, five winners of MacArthur fellowships, and two winners of the Fields Medal in mathematics. This suggests that the pattern for initiative is an important trait of the creative person, one that may be exhibited early in a person's career.

Drive for Originality

Since originality counts for so much in determining whether something qualifies as a truly creative solution, it wouldn't be surprising if creative people showed a particular drive to be original. Take, for example, the film student I encountered at Columbia College in Chicago who tells me he is satisfied only with stories that are unique unto him and offer something original to look at. In fact, when creative people were asked about what motivated them, respondents in Hayes's research who had been selected for their high levels of creative output were likely to answer, "To come up with something new."

This drive for originality has led creative people to pursue lifestyles that are an expression of their urge to be "authentic." Richard Florida, one of the early beacons in identifying the rising importance of the creative class, found that people who see themselves as creative "resist characterization as alternative or bohemian and insist that they are part of the culture, working and living inside it." Florida argues, in his book *The Rise of the Creative Class*, that the growing size of this population means that a certain amount of nonconformity makes for a new "norm-setting mainstream of society." As the culture moves closer to a full-blown renaissance, the society's tastes in everything from fashion to furniture will reflect an artful, high-design look that endows the user with a creative identity.

Flexibility

Creative people show a tendency to be flexible, especially when their ideas aren't working. In a study of 105 mathematicians who had been highly rated for creativity by other mathematicians, participants were asked to complete the California Psychological Inventory, which tests for flexibility, among other attributes. Those considered creative scored significantly higher than the rest on the flexibility scale.

Look no further than the dilemma of Ivan Pavlov for a good case in point. He was investigating the salivary reflex in dogs, who would salivate automatically when food was placed in front of them. The experiment went well at first, but after awhile, the dogs began to salivate before the food was placed in front of them. This development was not helpful to Pavlov's original purpose. However, rather than seeing it as a hurdle to be overcome, he saw it as a fascinating reaction. Rather than abandoning the work, he added variations to his experiments with the dogs. Against the advice of his colleagues, he brushed aside his original hypothesis and set a new goal for his work. This led to his breakthrough on the conditioned reflex, for which he eventually received a Nobel Prize.

Aspiration

It would be wrong to suggest that creation happens only when the creative person is in some sort of distress. Though this is true to an extent, there are other sorts of situations that lead to creation. In many cases, creators are taking advantage of opportunities to achieve an aspiration, or they recognize improvements that can be made. Whether an individual is exploring an opportunity or resolving a difficulty, the important point is that he or she is setting goals and initiating activities to accomplish those goals.

At the School of the Art Institute of Chicago, design students were asked to contribute a creative object to a furniture show in Milan. When the team assessed the environment in which their work would be placed, they saw a chaotic spectacle—the largest furniture fair in the world, where thousands of designers and manufacturers meet to exchange ideas and engage in commerce. They noticed that, amid all this intensity of visual input on the exhibits floor, there was no place to pause and reflect. Because the students aspired to a project that was both beautiful and practical, they hit on the idea of creating a place where show participants could retreat and refresh. They called their creation the Watershed, a resting spot that offers shelter, beauty, and refreshment. The design team used visualization and fabrication technology to lend a fluttering effect to the oversized leaf-like arms that enfold visitors into this quiet environment. Sensing technology helps the installation gently adjust to the users movements. Visitors feel a two-way exchange, making the experience both soothing and softly responsive.

Across the many sources Carnegie Mellon's Hayes explored, he found that goal setting and taking initiative are common traits among people who had been identified as creative. This implies an aspirational quality to creativity. In fact, in the cities my research team selected for their RenGen appeal, we typically encountered leaders who set ambitious goals and set about achieving them through painstaking efforts to build coalitions, as well as seeking partners and sponsors. Creative people not only aspire to be creative, they aspire, period.

Using Knowledge to Create

If we didn't know about PINGing, we might consider the formation of creative ideas as a right-brain process—an intuitive hit from out of the blue. In fact, eureka moments are problem-solving situations that typically involve ill-defined problems—that is, problems that cannot be solved unless the problem solver makes decisions or adds information of his or her own to clarify the problem.

Ill-defined problems often occur in practical settings. For example, in any design situation, the client typically specifies a few of the elements to be addressed within a specific budget and time frame, but the designer must contribute many more ideas before the design problem can be solved. The contributions can be references pulled from the storehouse and then adapted and nuanced.

What might be responsible for differences in people's ability to find problems or to PING? Among the speculations scholars have made over the years on this question, we can group the hypotheses this way:

- Extensive knowledge of a field increases the ability to recognize both opportunities and problems by analogy to previous experience. For example, if a chess situation resembles one the player has been in before, it could signal an opportunity if the previous outcome was favorable, and a problem if it was not.
- Knowledge outside of a field, acquired perhaps through hobbies or through switching professions, could provide a person with analogies not generally available to others in the field. Such analogies offer possibilities that other people from within the field might not see. That is why collaborative teams should include people from diverse fields.
- Strong evaluation skills lead a person to view problems in a way that minimizes their daunting aspects. The creator then can reassemble aspects of the problem and find patterns that suggest a new approach.

Framing the Problem Is Key

Since tasks that allow room for creativity are typically ill-defined, how a creative person frames the problem matters. A client of mine is a restaurateur who likes to place her eateries in vintage buildings, since that lends a certain charm and authenticity to the rustic Tuscan food that is her specialty. To outfit these places with a modern kitchen and dining room is a challenge. She relies on an architect, who is given specifications on the location, size, overall environment of the building, etc. To represent the design problem in sufficient detail so that it can be solved, the architect makes a great many decisions based on a rather ill-defined set of problems. Ill-defined problems offer a great deal of latitude in the way they can be represented or defined, and therein lies some of the reward for the creative person. For example, in one facility she decided that because of a neighboring shop, she needed a unique kind of entry. The architect also needs to make decisions about lighting, seating, the proximity of the bar to the kitchen, and how to configure floor space for maximum profitability. Galileo defined the problem of determining the velocity of light. He did not solve it. The formulation of a problem can be more critical than its solution, which might simply be a matter of mathematical skill or continued experimentation. In their book, *The Evolution of Physics*, Albert Einstein and Leopold Infeld wrote: "To raise new questions, new possibilities, to regard old problems from a new angle, requires creative imagination and marks a real advance in science." The way a person represents a task can have a critical impact on how hard the task is to accomplish, or even whether it can be accomplished at all. In a study of problem definition, subjects were given different representations of the same problem. The study showed that a problem represented one way may be sixteen times as hard to solve as the same problem represented a different way. The 16-to-1 range probably underestimates the full range over which changes in representation can contribute to a problem's difficulty.

Choosing to represent a problem visually rather than verbally, or choosing to represent the problem by one metaphor rather than another, can determine whether one person can solve the problem while another cannot. Hayes found that creative engineers tended to mix algorithmic and associative thinking and to represent knowledge both visually and symbolically. In other words, the creative person might be better at solving a problem because he or she was able to frame it in a way that it made it easier to solve.

Brandy Agerbeck is a graphic facilitator who helps corporate teams tackle complex problems in meetings where a lot of PINGing goes on. Big consulting firms such as Accenture and Ernst & Young use her services to help clients innovate. Rather than taking simple notes, she draws pictures and maps of the group's thought process so that participants can begin to visualize solutions.

I asked Brandy to explain how her work helps frame an ill-defined problem. She responded with an illuminating explanation, here in its entirety.

> Print is linear. Numbers are linear. Linear works well for instruction for building a persuasive argument, spinning a yarn. But problems and problem-solving are usually a tangle of many threads. They are complex and nuanced.
>
> Okay, so take a tangly, complicated problem and call a meeting to solve it. Get folks in a room together to talk about it. They may have an agenda. They talk for a predetermined amount of time and often don't get any further in solving the problem.
>
> Why? Well in a normal meeting, each person in the room is their own agent with their own agenda, their own hopes and frustrations. In most meetings, each person says what they have to say about the problem. Linear, linear, blah, blah, blah. "I think. . . ." "Well, I think. . . .", etc. Each person is their own thread, using a string of words to express themselves.

What I do is make maps of those conversations. While [all of] those folks are in the room talking at, around, and about a problem, I'm drawing what they are saying (and sometimes what they aren't saying) on a big piece of paper in front of them. Sounds simple enough, but what's important is that it works.

It helps a groups of individuals become a team of problem solvers. Here's why it works:

1. I'm integrating each person's linear speech into one, big spatial map of the conversation. Everyone can see the whole and the parts of the whole all at once. They can see where they are making progress and where they are stuck. It's all there in front of them, in ink on paper.

2. I'm using images and words and symbols and plenty of arrows. Words are super, but they can be strengthened and clarified when they are supported by memorable images and put in relationship to each other spatially.

3. I'm an outsider. Every other person in the room has their own pet projects they are championing, their own beefs with this man or woman or ideas about how it should be done. That's to be expected. We're all individual humans, who rarely work within organizations that truly encourage team problem-solving. I come in with my listening, thinking and drawing skills to serve the group and their conversation. But tomorrow, I go back to my company of one. Right now, I'm there to capture the conversation. I'm listening to everyone equally and getting the group's ideas up on the paper.

4. The process is completely transparent. And the object (the image) is tangible. There's no mystery to what I'm doing, because I'm doing it in real-time in front of people. I think the real power of the drawing is the verb—how it focuses people during the meeting, while they are processing. The bonus is that the drawing is also a noun—an artifact, something that represented where they were at that time.

What Brandy describes is a process for framing the problem. In her case, she draws pictures and captures brief phrases that guide people toward collective problem-solving, or at least collective clarity on what the true problem is. Most of us are undoubtedly familiar with the frustration of solving for the wrong problem and extending the innovation process. Defining the problem so others can see what to solve is an important discipline that talented people master in the RenGen.

Mastery

Mastery also plays an important role in problem definition. Studies show that a very important part of the difference between experts and novices may lie in the way they define the task to be performed. Hayes looked at writers and their editorial process. Novice writers tended to take a piecemeal approach, attacking each sentence separately, fixing the grammatical and spelling errors it contained and rarely paying attention to overarching problems such as coherence, flow, and impact of the whole text. The experts, on the other hand, were more concerned with the overall piece, although they fixed the specific errors, too. The experts did a far better job than the novices did, and it seems clear in this case that their better performance was a result of having defined a better task for themselves. One can't really expect to do a good job of revision with a task definition that ignores a very important class of problems.

While intelligence and motivation are both involved in creative performance, Hayes concludes that creative performance is more about the motivation of the creative person than about his or her mental abilities. Over time, this motivation improves the mental powers of creative people because they build large bodies of knowledge that contribute to creative performance, offering a broader reservoir of information to PING against. Put a different way, if a person is willing to work longer and harder than her peers, it's also likely that person will acquire a larger, more diverse body of information than others. In solving a problem, this extra information might be used directly to make an essential inference or might provide an analogy that would suggest a solution path.

Willingness to work hard could also lead to defining more intricate problems and setting higher standards for executing the solutions. Hayes reasons that higher standards lead creators to be more critical of their own work, and given their penchant for independence, they will set their own goals and hold themselves to a standard of originality that inspires them to reject goals that are commonplace or expected. This proves invaluable in crisis situations where the imperative is to solve ill-defined problems that are new. A prerenaissance environment is loaded with such problems. Finally, the motivation to be flexible makes it possible to change direction completely when a nuance presents itself, to sacrifice minor objectives to accomplish major ones, and to change the way a problem is framed to make progress.

It is important to understand how creativity works because the challenges we face have been building for decades and are complex enough to threaten our viability. However, our capacity to be creative in developing solutions for that crisis is increasing. Consider it Darwinian if you like, but consistent with the escalation of society's problems is an equally potent force for adapting: our ability to be creative.

CHAPTER FIVE

The Economics of the RenGen

A renaissance is a feast of art, innovation, and ideas. Having looked at the creative process that is fruitful in a renaissance, we also need to look at the way creative products are brought to market and consumed in such an environment. You may be wondering how big this market will be or how will it be structured. In this chapter, we will look at the economics of the RenGen, to assess its potential impact from perspective of the consumer, the producer, and the sponsor. We'll also consider the market structure that is taking shape for the RenGen—something having implications for future enterprise.

The Regulated and Deregulated Culture

For all its vigor, a renaissance is not a mosh pit of production, distribution, and consumption. There is a system in place that supports and structures those activities. In the Italian renaissance, for example, production and distribution were carefully controlled by the guilds that regulated the "who" and "how" of art practices. They did so primarily to ensure a healthy marketplace for both buyers and sellers.

Today, too, an elaborate infrastructure exists to regulate the production and consumption of creative work. Universities, museums, libraries, galleries, festivals, performing arts centers, art schools, publishing houses, and the traditional media—these all form a cosmos in which art and ideas circulate. This network is interdependent and has always had a great deal of power in confirming status: who is talented, what kind of art is important, what expressions should endure and be preserved. People who possess ideas outside this artistic and intellectual establishment have often been left out in the cold with their noses pressed against the glass, longing to be let inside the inner sanctum. A writer could submit a dozen novels before getting a bite from a publisher. A painter could languish for years without gallery representation.

The Internet has significantly lowered the barriers for talented individuals seeking an audience. But we must take into account that the amount of creative activity is such that bricks-and-mortar outlets for artistic expression are popping up everywhere. Today, in community arts centers, home studios, church basements, and living rooms, people are taking up everything from drawing to fiction writing and meeting regularly to produce and critique each other's work. Peter Steinhart, author of *The Undressed Art: Why We Draw* observes: "There are at least eighty different drawing groups meeting weekly in the San Francisco Bay Area. They range from very private gatherings of four or five artists in someone's living room to large drop-in sessions meeting once or twice a week in community centers. There are housewives' drawing groups and there are gay men's drawing groups—even a gay-men-drawing-naked group."

The city of Boston has tapped into the desire of everyday people to express their creativity. They host an annual sidewalk chalk-drawing festival that gives participating companies squares of sidewalk with their corporate name on each square. ArtStreet, the organization that manages the event, provides boxes of colored chalks so office workers can create a drawing. Companies send out individuals, or teams of employees, to chalk on the sidewalk. Often different departments in a company, or groups of employees, collaborate. Pedestrians vote on their favorite artworks by placing gold stickers on the chalk drawings. Artworks that inspire the most votes earn prize ribbons and recognition. Musicians, poets, and entertainers add a festival atmosphere throughout the lunch hour. In 2004, over 130,000 people attended the festivities.

Alongside the breakdown of traditional barriers experienced by artists and intellectuals is a wider category of activity across the common culture that is less concerned with the questions of who gets access to what and where. The common culture is moving toward a deregulated market for art and ideas where things like value and price will be arrived at based on a variety of public considerations and not dictated by a single authority.

The Setting of the Marketplace

"Which way to the market?" I asked the concierge at my hotel in Florence. She looked puzzled. I begged forgiveness for my halting Italian and we looked at a map together. Then I understood her quizzical look. Her finger pointed here and here and there and there. The "market" is everywhere. If you've traveled to Europe you know that the marketplace has often resided in a certain district of a town, or perhaps in a few places. Today, in cities like Florence, food, leather goods, clothing, housewares, art, and artifacts are available nearly everywhere, amidst the splendor of attractions like the Uffizi Gallery and the Duomo Cathedral. Now, to be sure, some of this commercial activity is what naturally occurs in tourist hot spots. Still, if you look at much older maps of Florence, even then markets were scattered about the city. As the cradle of the Renaissance, Florence was not only the center of production, but also the place where creative products could be readily acquired.

Despite the tomes of scholarly work written about the common culture of the first renaissance, we still consider the art of the period as something created for the public—a fresco or a statue. But large-scale public art is but a fraction of the overall output. Oxford historian Evelyn Welch explains it this way: "Any image belonged to a wider category of goods . . . which included liturgical and household furnishings, clothing, embroidery, maps, clocks, scientific and musical instruments—objects which all contributed to a general sense of contemporary and visual culture." He also notes that history has a way of elevating and making sacred even the most common daily objects from the Renaissance, "Objects, such as the metal plates known as paxes (meaning "peace" in Latin) which are now kept in untouchable glass cases, were once held, kissed, and wept over. Paintings and sculptures might be carried in processions, worn in hats, burnt in bonfires of luxury goods."

No more blatant example of art for consumption can be found than in the architectural models of the Church of St. Frances in Rimini; these were made of sugar and literally eaten.

How Big Is This Market?

It is one thing to look around our communities and notice that a lot of art and ideas are being generated. Translating that activity into reliable data is trickier. Still, some concrete numbers on size and scope of this rising renaissance can help in gauging its magnitude. We will first have a look at the numbers of people participating in the RenGen as producers and consumers, as well as examine how they are motivated by aspirations and values. Understanding people's motivations can make it clearer which attitudes might stick around in a changing world.

Today, we have sophisticated methods for gathering reliable numbers on the amount of activity in just about any aspect of the common culture. As a marketer, my initial impulse was to turn to a widely known outfit, AC Nielsen Company, the arbiters of mass media measurement, to find out how many cultural consumers there are in America. A former client of mine referred me to an earnest, quick-study of a man who picked up the phone on the first ring. I introduced myself and my research agenda. "I want to know more about the cultural consumer." He paused, "You know, I don't think we track that sort of thing. But it sounds like we should." He toyed with different angles on how we could get at that kind of information, and, as a consolation, he e-mailed me an in-house presentation on emerging consumer attitudes.

In the emergent state of the RenGen, the first stumbling block to measuring the indicative activity is being aware of the phenomenon in the first place. What comes next is just another of the statistical challenges we face in tracking emerging behaviors. For, as I would discover, getting at the size and scope of the growing interest in creative and cultural experiences would require some searching. And search I did for two years, to get the data that reveals the scope of producing and consuming creative products.

Here is what I uncovered: growth is coming from everywhere, fifth-graders to boomers, mostly female but increasingly male, and from coast to coast.

The Rise of the Cultural Consumer

Let's begin with the 12 million households that rank "avid book reading" as their number one leisure activity according to the Standard Rate and Data Service (SRDS), a company that collects data on consumer behavior for the advertising industry. Among its annual studies is a survey of more than 18 million U.S. households, from which it fashions lifestyle profiles. Richard Florida, author of *The Rise of the Creative Class*, counted 15 million workers, or 12 percent of the workforce who work in "directly creative activity" and form a "Super-Creative Core." Researchers Paul H. Ray and Ruth Anderson, in their rigorous book, *The Cultural Creatives*, estimate that some 50 million Americans fall into the category they call "cultural creatives." These are creative, optimistic millions who are, in Ray and Anderson's assessment, shaping a new kind of culture through personal values centered on curiosity about the world, self-reflection, and concern for the environment.

So how often do people have what they consider "cultural" experiences? Perhaps more so than you think. Here are some key findings from a national survey sponsored by the Wallace Foundation in 2004 on participation in the arts that tell the story:

- Nearly half of the general population attends cultural events **frequently**—once a month or more.
- The typical adult attends an average of **1.9** cultural events per month.
- Younger respondents (18–29) attend an average of **2.3** cultural events per month.
- Boomers (30–54) attend **1.8** cultural events per month.
- The mature segment (55+) attends an average of **1.7** cultural events per month.

Frequency of attendance shows a modest correlation with age, education, and income. Adults who have graduated from college, as well as those with incomes in excess of $75,000 per year, attend an average of 2.1 and 2.2 events per month, respectively.

It is a bias among many that the national interest in arts and culture is represented by a rich, but narrow vein, of the population. However, my research has convinced me that more and more Americans frequently take part in what can be considered artistic or creative activities. When asked in a market analysis about specific activities, most Americans (63%) said they frequently incorporate one to three artistic or creative activities in their lives, while 25 percent registered as high participators, frequently doing four or more. Estimates range between 30 and 12 percent of the population that do none. More than one third of the general public says they increased their attendance over the past year. From the more passive activities such as listening to music (76% do so frequently) to reading novels, poems, or nonfiction (66%), to drawing, painting, and needlework (24%) to playing an instrument or performing in some way (19%), Americans are involved in arts and culture.

It is one thing to look at major urban centers like New York and Los Angeles to calibrate the pulse of the rising RenGen. But I was just as curious about people living in cities like Anchorage, Atlanta, Chicago, Pittsburg, Seattle, and Philadelphia. Working with my colleagues, we burrowed into wide-ranging research from the Pew Charitable Trusts to Opera America to lend depth and breadth to our perspective. It led to some apple and oranges comparisons that are difficult to resolve completely. People in one city, for example, might consider a trip to Barnes & Noble a cultural happening if they decide to stay for an author reading, while research in other markets accounted for no such distinction.

The Explosion of Book Clubs

Reading for pleasure is the most accessible, democratic RenGen activity. With the robust proliferation of book clubs, more and more people are discovering reading as a social and intellectual activity. "We recently read *Crime and Punishment*, and everyone in our group, including a lawyer and a history major, brought something different to it," says Alma Oberst, a former journalism teacher who lives in Carmel, California. "Suddenly Dostoevsky came alive to me and seemed so relevant."

One book discussion group begets another. But since book clubs often sprout up informally, it is hard to get an exact statistic on how many are active. Rachel Jacobsohn, founder and president of the Chicago-based Association of Book Group Readers and Leaders, told us that there are approximately one million book clubs in America. They represent an array of combinations and themes as various as peoples' life situations and interests.

In 1998, Nancy Pearl, radio personality and author of the book *Book Lust*, recruited entire cities to read the same book at the same time. Her "One Book, One City" events were adopted by over forty U.S. cities including Los Angeles, Philadelphia, Seattle, and Chicago. Her novel idea of one city reading the same book at the same time has been, and continues to be, imitated in communities around the world. And the fanfare from these "One Book, One City" events has not only stimulated countless discussion groups, but also prompted businesses to get into the act by sponsoring book-related happenings, such as author appearances and at-work book discussion groups.

Interest in book clubs exploded in September 1996 when Oprah Winfrey launched her book club. It sparked a movement that had, and still has, people starting their own book clubs across the country. Many in the publishing business believe that Winfrey did for the book club what Elvis did for rock 'n' roll—she took it mainstream. Publishers were dubious at first that the public would respond when Ms. Winfrey chose serious literary fiction books for her club. However, her selections drove the publishers back to press to print more than 700,000 copies of literary titles. Book clubs continue to grow, and they are a form of leisure that is a good example of a RenGen pastime.

The Motivation to Consume

Despite all the unique and somewhat hard-to-categorize activity bubbling up, it is possible to distill the appeal of arts and culture down to four categories that represent a continuum of participation:

1. **Appreciation:** taking in the arts passively, such as listening to music and reading

2. **Attendance:** seeing performances and exhibitions, visiting libraries, museums, and arts festivals

3. **Expression:** doing arts such as creative writing, painting, music making, or drawing

4. **Aspiration:** projecting oneself into role of an artist or identifying with a creative aesthetic because it is associated with other qualities such as being creative, inner-directed

You very likely sat through an art appreciation course at some point in your life as a student. Just as my description suggests, you probably did so passively. In a revved-up market like the current one, it is possible to move across the spectrum from appreciation to expression in record time.

The Power of Aspiration

In 2001, the film adaptation of J.R.R. Tolkien's *Lord of the Rings* enthralled millions with its high-fantasy adventures of middle-earth. While the *Lord of the Rings* trilogy made household names of the artists associated with it, actor Viggo Mortensen used his celebrity to further his other creative interests—namely painting, photography, and poetry. Mortensen is a part-time musician, a published poet, and a photographer and painter whose work has been exhibited at art galleries such as the Robert Mann Gallery, Track 16 Gallery, Fototeca de Cuba, and Museet for Fotokunst in Denmark. To add to that, he founded the independent publishing house Perceval Press, named for the knight from the legend of King Arthur, to help other artists by publishing works that might not find a home in more traditional publishing venues.

What makes a film actor like Mortensen important at the rise of the RenGen is his power to inspire widespread appeal for creative pursuits among the mainstream. More specifically, it is a testament to the power of successful artists to evoke aspiration in others. In this way, Mortensen's publishing company works like a call-for-entries to aspiring writers who learn about him first, then seek his assistance to get their work known to a broader audience. This quality of aspiration plays an important role in a renaissance.

When Michelangelo and Leonardo da Vinci competed to win a prestigious commission for a fresco project that would depict a famous battle between the citystates of Pisa, it seemed that all of Florence was awaiting the outcome. By that time, the two artists had earned their reputations. Da Vinci was widely known as a great painter, having completed his masterpiece *The Last Supper* on the wall of a refectory in Milan. Michelangelo's towering statue *David* stood composed and complete on its pedestal behind the cathedral in Piazza della Signoria in Florence. For this competition, each sought to establish dominance over the other.

After working in secrecy for many months, the two artists emerged with their designs, each of which were over 1,000 feet of chalk drawings, known as cartoons, named for the outsized sheets of paper on which they were drawn. The reaction was immediate. As Ross King writes in his book, *Michelangelo and the Pope's Ceiling*: "Tailors, bankers, merchants, weavers, and of course, painters—all flocked to where the two cartoons were displayed." The works took on the proportion of "historic relics" visited by hundreds and discussed by many more. Whether in a high renaissance, or at the beginning point of its emergence, master talent comes to the fore and inspires everyday people to join in the excitement. Some come to hear about it, others to witness, and yet others to study and pick up their own pens and dip them into ink.

Meet the VIVIDS:
Voracious Independent Visual
and Inner-directed Cultural Consumers

Every market has a "sweet spot"—that core group of followers that form its base. The RenGen is no different. Depending on which subsection of the demographic we examine, we will find a core set of values such as freedom of expression and interest in work that conveys an original point of view. What may differ are certain tastes and preferences that are dictated by the practicalities of age, gender, and income.

Some people "gotta have art." They are the core of the cultural consumer segment and they are loyal. Painting a portrait of a VIVID involves melding data from a variety of sources: my team looked at market research from *The New Yorker* magazine's readership panel, along with audience research from major institutions such as the Seattle Opera Company, the New York Philharmonic, and the Art Institute of Chicago's members, NPR listeners, and user data from large urban libraries. Anecdotally, I have encountered VIVIDs and even interviewed some of them for this book. What emerges is a *type*. This is not to be confused with a stereotype. Consider the following composite that illustrates the personality.

Portrait of a VIVID

Let me introduce you to Margaret K. You can find her at an opening night gala of a regional theatre company, volunteering for her church's music department, or sweeping through a museum on her way to an appointment. She rises early and runs every morning without fail. She once trained as a dancer. After having children, she began writing fiction as an outlet for her creative drive. Despite her 40-something age, her appearance has a timeless quality—very little makeup to detract from skin born of great genes and pricey department store creams.

Margaret is generous and curious, optimistic and smart. In case you feel tempted to make assumptions about her status, I will tell you straight out: she is not a snob. Nor does she use her love of the arts as a weapon of class warfare. It is simply her passion and she indulges it with gusto. Her radio dial is tuned to National Public Radio. She watches PBS—but only selectively since she finds some of the programs too tame. Mortgage, clothes, housewares, insurance, lawn services, and tuition are all payments controlled by her. She buys her cars new, not used. Minus donations, she spends more than $3,500 annually on cultural experiences. When she travels, she'll spend more, and it will be to experience the culture of a place. In fact, she will spend three times more than the average tourist. She is more willing to purchase products from companies who sponsor the arts, and she claims to "trust" them more than companies that do not. Her modest art collection features a Picasso drawing and two Serrano photographs.

She associates with others like herself, and she entertains often in her home. Unfailingly self-directed, friends admire her and seek her advice.

People like Margaret attend four cultural events monthly. Movies and visits to museum art exhibitions are equally popular, followed by live drama/theater, art galleries, and music. VIVIDs attend events at a higher rate than the general public, with one exception—popular music at large venues. Art is life-enhancing because it provides a sense of belonging. They are passionate about their belief in arts as a source of community pride and they consider the role of cultural institutions important to fostering creativity and appreciation of the arts. They will financially contribute to cultural institutions to preserve resources, expose patrons to new things, provide enjoyment, and improve the quality of life.

Thrill and challenge are often what's in it for VIVIDs when it comes to experiencing art. They draw a sense of belonging from learning about other cultures, connecting with their cultural roots through the arts. Finally, they are drawn to quality and find it important to experience the "great" or "important new works."

They also lust after information. They buy books, research artists, and explore world music. They use the Internet and tap their network of friends for recommendations of books, music, and cultural events far in excess of the general public. The value of invitations from friends and family members is critical—not publicity or reviews from critics—and they consider "being in the know" about new productions and books an important social responsibility. Many of them would qualify as the "mavens" that Malcolm Gladwell describes in his influential book, *The Tipping Point*. People like Margaret are also well educated. The incidence of postgraduate degrees is staggering among this group compared with the general population. Because the amount of education often correlates to income, it is therefore not surprising that these individuals are affluent, with household incomes often topping $150,000. That is, unless they are artists themselves—in which case, they share similar values and engage in similar consumption patterns with art, but do so "on the cheap," using low-budget services such as libraries and museums on free days, and attending shows as guests of fellow artists.

As the RenGen undercurrent picks up momentum, the collective mind-set will be the mother of all psychographics—crossing gender, income, and even ethnic divides. What RenGenners share are the same expressive qualities, an inner-directness, and appreciation for visual and creative experiences. Some marketers have focused solely on people like Margaret K., who can easily afford higher-end accouterments to her RenGen lifestyle, and therefore missed the much-larger and growing portion of the market. The rising tide is the younger, edgier, and more technologically attuned RenGenners who are defining a new social order.

The Indie Movement Becomes a Social Construct

A renegade movement has been quietly growing among artists and it is looking to topple the twin pillars of the mainstream creative world: music and film, which heretofore have been guarded by industry moguls. Emboldened by the facilitating medium of the Internet, encouraged by their use of iPods, and educated at art schools and universities, the members of this renegade movement have quickly multiplied to form the "indie" phenomenon. The concept of "indie" anything is key to understanding the overall RenGen market, as it affects production, distribution, market structures, and consumption.

The term *indie* can be loosely defined as the production and distribution of a creative work by means other than the established "system." Hollywood has a system. Record companies and publishers have a system. The indie approach is decidedly grassroots and free-range. Using the Internet to amplify word-of-mouth allows artists to build an audience without traditional power tools such as capital and clout. Indie in any genre always implies the same thing: it is work produced and brought to market outside the formal "system."

Today, the indie movement is represented in film, music, and publishing. It's greatly facilitated by technology, in particular the Internet. Taken together, it is also fair to say that the indie identity has become a social construct.

Take the example of Eric V., a 17-year-old high-schooler living in Chicago. He belongs to the school's art club. His science fair project was an original animated short film about cell mitosis. Upon graduation, Eric plans to attend art school to study filmmaking and graphic design. As a consumer, Eric prefers things that are authentic and set him apart. But he has a habit of recruiting his friends to join him, so they buy what he buys and they form a group of "indies" making a statement. Eric was the first to own Blackspot shoes, with a hand-drawn red dot at the toe for "kicking corporate ass," as the slogan declares. The makers of Blackspot shoes have built an explicitly nonbranded shoe with a black spot where a logo would go. The shoes are produced in small, non-sweatshop factories, using non-animal-based and recycled materials such as old tires. They are marketed online and through the homegrown publication of the shoes' inventors, *The Adbusters*, an independently operated, anticorporate magazine headquartered in Vancouver, Canada. The result is the ultimate "indie" product.

Indie Art Becomes an Entre-prise

As technology lowers the barrier to entry, more aspirants will seek out a piece of the action, in some cases lured by sponsors who want to extend the indie momentum. For an example, look no farther than the deal where the *New York Times* joined forces with indieWIRE to present "Undiscovered Gems," an eight-month-long film series that runs in twelve markets across the country and is being presented in association with the California Film Institute. The audience votes for its favorite film to win a cash award of $50,000 for the filmmaker; theatrical release in New York, Los Angeles, and at least five other U.S. cities during 2007; as well as an exclusive broadcast on Sundance Channel. The partnership will bring one film per month to theaters in at least eleven cities.

The indie film genre alone has gotten so much attention that its very authenticity is threatened. This is a significant challenge, since "keeping it real" is the lifeblood of the indie attitude.

The early investors in the movement wonder if all the attention will be too much and the idealistic center of the movement will groan under the weight mainstream traffic. Sundance Film Festival founder Robert Redford put it this way in 2006: "To the outside world, it's a big fat market where you have people like Paris Hilton going to parties. Now, she doesn't have anything to do with anything. I think the festival is close to being out of control."

But what if Redford is wrong? What if the universe can expand to contain the ordinary people who comprise the mass audience? The research tells us that the public already likes indie personalities and their products, especially when they are from someone with a sense for what is popular and entertaining, like Quentin Tarantino.

The point is that something once considered esoteric, edgy, and artsy has become an assiduously followed and heavily marketed cultural offering. Today, independent film still lacks a colossal mass audience of blockbuster Hollywood products—in 2006, the Tribeca Film Festival claimed only 150,000 audience members in New York. It is true that the audience for home rentals of indie works is considerably larger, and there are occasional runaway hits such as *The Blair Witch Project* or *Good Will Hunting* that achieve broader distribution into local theaters and hence enjoy mass audiences. However, the scope of the audience that attends screenings at film festivals has little to do with the aspirational audience. The latter is where the action is and those numbers are growing. The art of filmmaking at the rough-and-tumble independent level is being adopted by the culture as a social construct to which people aspire. Therein lies its power. And if the popularity holds and it retains its renegade chic, an important benchmark will be reached in gauging the reach of the RenGen.

Indie Engages the Power of Aspiration

Nowhere in the art world is the power of aspiration more evident than in independent film. A 2005 study by the *New Yorker* magazine and the LaPlaca Cohen Agency revealed that film festivals, the common venue for independent film screenings, are attended by a scant 2.3 percent of the general public with any frequency. Consider that in the same study 68.3 percent of the public expressed interest in independent film—and that film was the overall most popular cultural event among the general public. So while few people actually attend the most direct sources of indie film, venues like Sundance or Tribeca Festivals, both are widely known and earn high levels of media attention.

The dawn of home video helped to grow an audience for genres like foreign film and American-made documentaries. As Peter Biskind writes in his book, *Down and Dirty Pictures*: "By the mid-1980s, indie films were starting to build an identity and an audience. Grosses spiraled upward. *Kiss of the Spider Woman* racked up a very sweet $17 million." According to *American Demographics*, as of 2001, The Independent Film Channel had a subscriber base of 30 million households, and surprisingly, subscribers are more likely to live in middle markets such as St. Louis, Orlando, and Phoenix, rather than New York or Los Angeles. Even though only 2.3 percent of the population attend film festivals, which is the entry point for most independent exhibition, the media attention fuels mass consumerism—as evidenced in home video and home subscribership.

As interest increases, the landscape grows more fertile across the supply and delivery chain. In the last decade, the number of independent films being released into theatres has doubled. In 2001, Landmark Theaters opened The Renaissance Place in Highland Park, Illinois, a Chicago suburb. Located in a retail development alongside Pottery Barn and Eddie Bauer, this suburban multiplex screens independent features and foreign films. Taken collectively, this accessibility helps cultural consumers go beyond a vague awareness of independent film and into full-blown appreciation.

With the intensifying media spotlight on independent film—not to mention its increased accessibility via companies like the Sundance Network and Miramax—the genre verges on becoming mainstream enough to potentially drive off the early adopters, those who relish the unbridled frontier.

Nonetheless, the aspirational pull of indie film (or indie anything) should continue to gain traction, as part of the idealism that is a feature of the RenGen mind-set. Actor Edward Norton (as quoted in *Down and Dirty Pictures*) recalled his days after college when he ran into a classmate who got cast in the low-budget feature *The Brothers McMullen*. Actors took these risks to gain experience and get a piece of the action. At Sundance, the film won hearts, minds, and a distribution contract. Norton says, "I was twenty-two. There was a sense that anything was possible . . . there was this vortex that you could head toward that had nothing to do with Hollywood, the sense that, holy shit, some kid with $25,000 from his parents could end up at Sundance

Film Festival." Plainly, more breeds more. When the formal barriers to entry can be gotten around, and more aspirants are being
stimulated to produce more work, you have what we now face:
the early stage of a renaissance.

Production of Creative Work

I pressed my way through the heavy bronze doors of the old Car-
son Pirie Scott Building that architect Louis Sullivan designed.
I was in search of the site of the new interdisciplinary architecture and design department at the School of the Art Institute
of Chicago. After a few wrong turns amid the hustle and debris
of construction, I found Tony Jones, the school's president. The
decades of running a prestigious art school, which Jones likens
to directing "an unrehearsed circus," have not dimmed his disposition. As someone who oversees one of the handful of art
colleges that consistently produce world-class artists, Mr. Jones
has insight into the production side of art and design. From his
perspective, there is good news and bad news.

The good news is that the numbers of applications to the school
are up—way up—which suggests that productivity is up and will
continue to grow even more, as a greater number of artists enter
the market. The not so good news is that the interest in studying
art and design is so vigorous that other institutions are jumping
into the arena and competing with new art and design programs.

Jones says the number of applicants has grown 30 percent
domestically in the last two years, and 40 percent from international applicants. "We see extremely talented, very bright young
artists. But we also see mature people looking to at last claim

their creative destiny. They are smart and organized and have done a great deal of thinking about how they want to use their talent." The national figures tell the same story.

A Growing Movement

According to College Board data, training for a creative pursuit is hot. There was a 44 percent increase from 1996 to 2005 in the number of high school seniors who say that they plan to major in visual and performing arts. Comparatively, the increase in intended business and commerce majors was a more modest 12 percent, while the percentage of those who plan to major in social sciences and history has decreased by 15 percent. Data on ACT takers show the same pattern, according to Richard Hessel, a principal with the Art & Science Group. "In 1997, 45,344 students specified visual and performing arts as an intended major," he says. "In 2005, 60,666 stated an intention to major in visual and performing arts, an increase of 33.7 percent." This demand has made for new and innovative additions to the traditional art school curriculum to keep pace with demand, not to mention the technology-driven arts such as video, graphic design, and fashion arts.

Seizing the momentum, Tony Jones is building a center for innovation at the Art School of Chicago, supported in part by the Motorola Company to honor a long-time employee and inventor of the Razr phone who died of cancer. The center will allow the School to collaborate with companies, from automakers to office furnishing manufacturers, to experiment with various ideas and new media in order to tackle real design problems (for example, "how to make a better pair of scissors" for an aging, arthritic society). Students want to design products that are eco-friendly or help solve larger social problems, Jones tells me, and this ethos is a driving ambition for many of his graduate students in particular.

In their early thirties, these students come to learn specific skills, and they work in talented teams to harness their ambitions into creating something functional. "There will always be the lone artist toiling away in his garret," Jones tells me. "But we see less and less desire to be that kind of artist." Now, artists need to learn the social skills of collaboration if they expect to thrive. Since much of the new media is technological, artists and designers develop highly specialized skills. To attack a complex design problem, such as designing a safer, smaller car for urban settings, a diverse team of specialists need to pool their ideas. For people in education and management, this business of being socialized toward collaboration is a growing area need.

Looking around the School of the Art Institute of Chicago, it is hard to picture a parent blithely handing over a check for $35,000 for a year's tuition and fees without asking themselves a few questions about health and safety. Gritty and frayed at the edges in some spots, the school has the feel of a 24-hour restaurant—always foot traffic, always something to pick up or mop up. In one room, a young woman sits on the floor busily sewing glittering beads onto a bra. Her eyes, with darkly smudged mascara rings, show signs of an all-nighter. Her needle moves in and out of the fabric. I ask her what she's working on. "My final project in fashion design. It's killing me. I had no idea how hard it would be or I would have chosen a different design." I step closer to look at her handiwork. I tell her it looks great, eye-popping, I say. "Yeah, I think it'll be fine, but it's still killing me."

For all this work, passion, and expense one might hope for some measure of attainment for these artists. Yet, the odds of all this effort leading up to a paying career in the arts are dismal. One art teacher reckoned that only 4 percent of art school graduates work as artists. Still, their passion for the experience seems hard to squelch.

The outpouring of creativity may not be driven by consumer appetites for more products in the art market. Some argue that the desire to create is drawn from within and is innate. Others say it is driven by those who set out to build their careers around being creative, and when the marketplace cannot absorb the volume of output, trained artists look elsewhere for opportunity. Often, they look for jobs where they can do meaningful work and use some facet of their talents. As more and more companies look to build businesses on the basis of intellectual property, entertainment, travel, and information, these "re-artists" will prove valuable. Starbucks, for example, already sees the value of hiring artists, especially creative Type A personalities. In 2005, I attended a marketing workshop where an executive from Starbucks spoke, and he explained the training philosophy at Starbucks by explaining their hiring philosophy. "If we hire creative Type As we have much less training to do." This was especially true when it came to customer service—the hallmark of Starbucks, he explained.

The value of artistically trained employees also rings true for companies like BRC in Burbank, California. BRC is in the edutainment business. It designs high-concept museum exhibitions and entertainment spaces incorporating live actors, special effects, and animation to create the experience.

In a café in the Los Feliz district of Los Angeles, I sat down to talk with Mark Hayward, a young executive at BRC. The company recruited Hayward from the Museum of Science and Industry in Chicago. Coincidentally, he is a graduate of the School of the Art Institute of Chicago and is the kind of guy who could succeed in sales or advertising, but who chose art for its wide-open spaces that let him design his own ticket. Polished and upbeat, Hayward confides that BRC couldn't survive without the large pool of artistic people it can draw from, many of them lured to Los Angeles by the movie business. "The city is a magnet for creative people, and we need a wide range of talents to run of company like this," he says.

The story goes something like this: An aspiring filmmaker ends up needing to make the rent; she takes a job at BRC because it pays well and she can still use her talent on projects that have an educational purpose. As the knowledge economy continues to churn, companies like BRC will find opportunity. And better still, it will be first in line to cherry-pick some of the best creative talent.

A New Business Model for Patronage

Much as businesses are becoming the patrons of RenGen artists—even if through an employment contract versus an artistic commission—a new patronage model is also emerging to support the production and consumption of independent art.

These are companies whose businesses are looking to harness some of the indie allure for their brands. BMW and Skyy Vodka have departments that commission and produce their own films. They hire young filmmakers who might otherwise take years to break into the business, and the resulting short productions are made available 24/7 online. Chrysler sponsored its very own "virtual film competition" under the auspices of the Chrysler Film Project. For the RenGen, there is no apparent stigma associated with corporately funded artmaking—just as long as the resulting product is judged as being authentic and artful. It's a reasonable alternative to the slow grind of the more bureaucratic "system" and the high-risk hand-to-mouth lifestyle that is the indie market.

Take the case of Spike Lee. Arguably one of independent film's most celebrated artists, Lee took a job at DDB Needham Advertising where he led an urban marketing unit called Spike/DDB. The agreement called for him to direct urban-oriented commercials for a variety of clients. He previously worked with DDB on an educational spot for the College Fund/United Negro College Fund. Artists of the RenGen will move in and out of commercial work to gain important experience, not to mention contacts for future patronage and employment. Rather than seeing this as "selling out," the RenGen see commercial work as yet another alternative to the stiff restraints of the traditional intellectual/literary/artistic establishment.

Sacred Ground—The Institutions that Support Production and Distribution

Our established institutions—arts centers, libraries, museums, and universities, along with the tax dollars and patron capital that supports them—are critical distribution points for creative products. They contribute a great deal to growing the audience of consumers. The public believes the role of cultural institutions is to entertain, preserve important art, and expose people to new things. In surveys, people associate these venues with concepts of improving oneself and being inspired. VIVIDs see things more broadly. They believe that the arts improve the quality of life because having a robust arts scene defines quality for a community and inspires creativity among the populace.

In the 1980s, cultural institutions faced draconian budget cuts from government agencies. This was followed by the "culture wars" of the 1990s when Senator Jesse Helms led an impassioned struggle to defund, and hence dismantle, the National Endowment for the Arts. He succeeded in changing the rules of the game by imposing strict guidelines about what kind of content would be funded and reducing the government's contribution to the NEA.

To defend its flanks, the art world set about justifying its relevance by proving there was an economic value to the arts. Bottom-liners were fed data and research abstracts that proved culture creates jobs and drives business to other merchants. And there is truth to those arguments.

In 2002, my firm interviewed a modest sampling of twenty business owners in Chicago. We talked to restaurant owners, retailers, and hotel managers who were able to describe the positive impact on their businesses during pre- and postshow timeframes, as theatre goers sought to extend their evenings. The economic argument was furthered by Richard Florida in *The Rise of the Creative Class*, where he argued that cities with lots of great art and cultural infrastructure provide a delectable backdrop for creative worker bees to live, work, and play. Since this talent is attractive to many cities, the argument is that it's worth it to maintain museums, performance spaces, and good libraries for the public, just to keep a vibrant lifestyle for those whom Florida sees as the pre-eminent breadwinners in the knowledge economy: the creatives.

In 2005, the Rand Corporation probed deeper into this topic with its own study on the value of arts and culture in the United States. Rand researchers concluded that the benefits fell into two categories: intrinsic and instrumental. The intrinsic aspects help us grow our intellectual and creative capacity; they inspire, entertain, and reassure us in otherwise uncertain times. The instrumental have to do with job creation, urban revitalization, and spillover economic benefits to sympathetic commercial entities.

The Rand study argues that the civilization flourishes when both benefits are recognized so as to "enrich the public sphere." In other words, some of the value is softer—it is social, emotional, and cognitive. Bottom-liners may be tempted to dismiss this element. But there is a growing movement toward trusting in what is unseen, and accepting that some experiences transcend what can be measured by experts. This is evidenced by the number of psychologists and anthropologists who now work for major advertising agencies and are charged with the task of uncovering deep-seated human motivations that often defy outright quantification.

What Lies Ahead

Americans prize the contribution of art to one's quality of life and to the education and development of its youth. However, research shows that Americans associate early exposure to creative activity with another benefit—that of understanding other peoples and cultures, something that is a key driver in our global, outsourced economy. More impressive is that the sentiment is universal, crossing over gender, ethnicity, and economic status. It even scored high among first-generation immigrants. The fact that there is a statistically significant relationship between believing that the arts contribute to the education and development of children and also agreeing that the arts promote the understanding of other people and cultures foretells a sense of "openness." This openness is such a feature in the renaissance mind-set. In a global economy, the most important benefits bestowed by the creative output may in fact be indirect ones. Your kid may not be the next Virginia Woolf, but can she think like Virginia Woolf? Golden.

In this atmosphere, the creative fervor we are witnessing is a testimony to the rise of the next renaissance. Toting up the numbers, we have to conclude that all this creative activity—whether it be production or consumption—constitute the kind of broad-based socioeconomic phenomena that should make economists take notice and marketers plot strategy. More important, all this industry radiates energy that, as it builds up, penetrates the rest of the society, including its most dynamic organizations.

CHAPTER SIX

The Mind's Eye—Meet the RenGen Aesthetic

Style is important in a renaissance. Look and feel matter a great deal, as do the sensations associated with things and places. There are several reasons why the RenGen want to live in a supersensory world of objects and places. Writers like Virginia Postrel, author of *The Substance of Style*, believe that design is an expression of identity. There is some truth to that. But in the consumer-centric American consciousness, there has always been interest in products designed to proclaim personal identity, so aesthetics as self-validation is well-tilled topsoil. To comprehend the need for the RenGen to experience life-enhancing atmospherics from even the most mundane situations, such as shopping at Target, we must consider the RenGen aesthetic as part of the changing mind-set.

Aesthetics experts place more value on perception than intellect. It is as if the look and feel of things in our environment takes on heightened power to prompt our actions. Because our use of the word *aesthetic* refers to a set of values and guidelines for favoring one thing over another, the aesthetic becomes an organizing principle in a capitalistic society.

The hallmarks of an aesthetic are:

1. It creates **distinction** from the ordinary and the undifferentiated perceptions that blend into the environment unnoticed.

2. It has a **cutting edge**. Some things make the cut and others do not, but there is clarity as to why something has value among a specific group of people.

3. It **persists** over a significant period of time.

The RenGen embraces a more comprehensive universe of ideas and sensory relationships. In other words, aesthetics and cognition work together like form and function. In an earlier chapter, we looked at how scientists approached researching brain function. They took a decidedly "whole" brain approach, accounting for things like observation, perception, logic, memory recall, and imagination as a system. I'll rely on this same integrated approach to the RenGen aesthetic because it helps express the "cultural mentality" that is emerging.

As Pitirim Sorokin observes in his monumental study of civilizations, *Social and Cultural Dynamics*, "cultural mentality" propels new ideas of what is significant and what is no longer relevant. The RenGen aesthetic explains plenty, but most important it reveals an important facet of how RenGen individuals, whether they are 45-year-olds or teenagers, will materialize meaning in the world.

A Change in Perspective

A shift in perspective is often manifested in the art of a culture. When the common culture undergoes a breakthrough in new understanding, it is accompanied by a change in people's idea of good design. This is typically followed by rapid mastery where new techniques help many artists render designs that evoke the new perspective.

In the first renaissance this shift was very literal—artists discovered visual perspective. The theory of perspective boils down to the apparent size of an object decreasing as the distance from the eye increases. It's the phenomenon that makes railroad tracks appear to converge in the distance. The flat rigidity of the Byzantine world gave way to pictures of human figures with rounder features and bigger eyes, situated in lush natural settings where the fields diminished in the horizon, thus representing a multi-dimensional view of the world. Nature and people's place in it were meant to be fully understood, and therefore had to be fully depicted by artists.

The use of visual perspective allowed people to imagine there was something beyond the horizon. But it also gave way to a shift in values. In the early days of the Renaissance that straddled the Byzantine world, the value of the artwork lay in its materials. Chalices, picture frames, home altars, and statues of saints were prized very early on for the precious materials from which they were made. Walk through the Metropolitan Museum in New York City or the Uffizi Gallery in Florence and you'll see that there is no end to the number of solid gold and emerald- and ruby-encrusted artifacts from the early Renaissance.

That rich style persisted throughout the Renaissance, but was eventually challenged by an interest in beauty over luxury. Eventually, people realized that no amount of luxurious materials would mask a poorly conceived piece of art, and a piece with a captivating design might fetch a high price on that basis. As the

Renaissance spread its aesthetic into the most common of house-holds, and as the techniques of artists grew more sophisticated in conveying the emotions and humanity of their subjects, people came to treasure the design of the piece as much as or more than its materials. As Evelyn Welch writes in *Art and Society in Italy 1350–1500*, "The presentation of a set of majolica plates or vases could be received with as much rapture as if they had been made of gold." In this situation, imagination and utility trump the indulgence of luxury that says more about wealth than imagination.

Fusion: The Catalytic Energy of a RenGen

If we can say the twentieth century was catalyzed by fission—the splitting up of the nuclei—then the RenGen era is characterized by fusion—the process by which multiple nuclei are drawn together to form a heavier nucleus. This is accompanied by the release of energy. Everywhere our research team looked we found evidence of fusion. The coming together of two unlikely pairings can result in unusual, but useful, new things or ideas. This fusion contributes to the aesthetic in observable ways.

Examples of fusion include:

Edutainment. Take, for example, the Bellagio Hotel in Las Vegas. A casino fused with an art museum produces adult fun (gambling) in a setting that is educational and inspirational. The renowned Boston Museum of Fine Arts once loaned paintings from its collection to the Bellagio, bestowing on the hotel and casino an irrefutable pedigree.

Organized religion fused with new spiritualism. Renaissance people lived in an insecure world of religious factionalism, war, surprise attacks, and assassinations. In that unstable world, paradoxes existed everywhere. Psychics competed with clerics for moral authority. Pope Julius had a papal astrologer who advised him on dates to launch projects and hold celebrations. People in a renaissance are able to fuse disparate spiritual truths into one set of beliefs that they can hold in their imaginations.

Capitalism fused with social work to create cause-related marketing. Once a concept that companies used to create a point of difference, cause-related marketing will become pervasive for the RenGen. The RenGen will expect every purchase they make to do some good, cure a disease, or clean up the environment. Cause-marketing will be the entry fee for playing in the marketplace at all.

Some businesspeople believe they must covertly evoke certain positive associations with their brands by manipulating the senses; however, thinking this way may be overcomplicating their work. The bigger opportunity in the fused world is to present an offering that solves a problem, does some good, and delivers aesthetically. This relieves the customer of any cognitive dissonance caused by the thought that his purchase is too one-dimensional, accomplishing nothing more than a simple, selfish transaction.

With this as a backdrop, let's uncover how the RenGen mindset is coaxing other aesthetic changes in the common culture.

The will to be reborn

As described earlier, the desire to "make me new again" drives everything from Botox to evangelism. For people of the RenGen, the idea of reconstructing themselves—physically and spiritually—becomes an expression of rebirth.

The exaltation of roots

Throughout this book, I make the case that a renaissance is not the same as a revolution. Although the innovations that spring from the period can revolutionize the way we do things, a renaissance builds on history instead of overturning it. As a result, people develop a fascination for the traditions and articles of the past. Historians agree on this point. Both the Italian Renaissance and today's emerging RenGen share the fascination with roots, even in the broadest, most sweeping sense, such as in our common ties to ancient peoples and customs. Ancient forms and iconography come to the forefront in a renaissance. Symbols, icons, logos, and pictures that tell stories will be the predominant form of communications. The emphasis will be on visual and aural representation of ideas. Why? Because they can be experienced as well as intellectually derived.

Devotional love expressed in objects

Art is both sacred and useful. People in a renaissance wear their art on hats and shirts, display it on flags, and exhibit it in devotional areas of their homes lit by candles. Prayer beads are a fashion accessory, and even the body, the most functional form we inhabit, becomes a canvas.

Rapid expansion of building and types of building materials

Whether because of the decline preceding a renaissance that brings with it a degradation of property and housing, or the expansion of population in certain regions, namely, the "second" cities, there is during a renaissance a building boom that attracts artists, architects, and craftsmen to feed the demand of a broad population who appreciates decorative art.

A respect for knowledge

This is more about the aggressive exchange of ideas than the rote textbook memorization many of us were schooled in. Knowledge becomes more accessible, and authoritarian experts are replaced by all forms of apprenticeship and collaborative exchanges that may serve a utilitarian function (for example, building a farmer's market in the center city) but have the benefit of teaching all the participants new skills and methods.

The elevation of human potential

Some form of inner-directedness is present in the context of a rebirth. Enlightenment and understanding become the business of everyone, not just the elites. Humanism argues that it is up to the individual person to attain enlightenment, as each is fundamentally capable. Life coaching, motivational books, career planning, self-help, and advice for maintaining mental and physical health continue to converge with more religious and even business management discourse.

The Virtues of the Flawed

What we see when we look at the world is interpreted first emotionally, then rationally. The sped-up pace of our lives forces us to interpret what we are sensing and then feeling and to find ways to cogently deal with it in ever more brief snippets. Coping in such an environment means accepting limitations. I am reminded of a recent situation involving my 82-year-old mother. An immigrant and a big believer in doing things right, she called one day with an unsettling question. "I am not sure what to do with my

180 shares of General Motors stock if they go bankrupt. Should I cash them in or forget it?" she asked. I was dumbstruck.

Having grown up in the Motor City, the idea of General Motors going bankrupt is not something anyone ever imagined possible. As a kid, everyone on my block made their living from the auto industry and, in particular, GM. I witnessed Lee Iacocca resurrect Chrysler and become a television star in the process. In short, GM was bedrock never to be shaken.

My mother's question helps introduce an important lesson RenGenners have internalized: nothing is permanent. They didn't learn it by paying attention to the stock ticker or the nightly business report or the *Wall Street Journal*, but by looking out the window. It is a sensibility that translates directly into a specific aesthetic.

RenGenners, with their focus fixed on the natural world, have developed respect for its power along with a mature appreciation for our inability to control things such as the weather, let alone predict it through technology. A decade of early springs, snowless winters, floods, hurricanes, and tidal waves has made an impression on the RenGen psyche. To help explain the effect of nature on the RenGen way of thinking, I'll flavor my observations with some in Leonard Koren's brief and digestible 2004 book, *Wabi-Sabi for Artists, Designers, Poets, & Philosophers*. Japanese Wabi-Sabi is a design approach of growing influence that relies heavily on the natural world unadorned.

The planet has taught the RenGen three lessons that are imprinted in the RenGen mind-set:

1. **Permanence is an illusion.** Everything breaks down to nothingness. Extinction and rebirth are the inevitable cycle of life. Even things that look solid break down: rock, steel, stars,

ideas, texts, proofs, and art all decline, fade away, and fall into oblivion.

2. **Nothing is perfect.** Even on close inspection, the most flawless objects are flawed. Security systems are breachable, viruses cannot be contained by universal inoculation, and, whether we are talking about diamonds or tempered steel, flaws are unavoidable.

3. **All things are incomplete.** There is never an ending and beginning to anything. We can decide that enough has been done, said, or written about something. But that is a self-imposed demarcation.

Before I go any further to explain how the Wabi-Sabi aesthetic is showing up in the RenGen, let me first give you a glimpse into how the ethos of Wabi-Sabi is realized in objects. Andrew Juniper, an expert on Wabi-Sabi design, who describes a metal bowl that caught his eye in a Turkish restaurant and he bartered to purchase it: "The small dark bowl that had so caught my eye had no real design to speak of. The glazed surface was rich with visual nuance and its simple, unrefined form was pure and unaffected . . . it was extraordinarily expressive with the imperfections and impermanence of life." These are subtly innate characteristics. Japanese culture as a whole leans toward subtlety. Even sword makers speak of the "soul" of the blade, which is imbued with a somewhat mystical aura. It would be a mistake, though, to consider the Wabi-Sabi aesthetic accidental or haphazard. It is *purposeful* in its stripping away of artifice to get to the essence of something.

Interestingly, the Wabi-Sabi had its rise in 1300—the beginning of the first renaissance in Europe. The term Wabi-Sabi suggests qualities of humility and looks to nature for its inspiration.

It is the antithesis of the starched rigors of Western culture that strive for perfection.

Popular culture in the United States for the last twenty years has venerated a Martha Stewart aesthetic of idealized perfectionism. But the RenGen is shifting toward an aesthetic that is decidedly more Wabi-Sabi. It shows up on the fringes of fashion and in high-end advertising that is aimed at people like graphic and interior designers. Wabi-Sabi has persisted through history perhaps because its message is pure. It strikes a chord that affirms our sense of belonging to a natural realm that anchors us in an otherwise uncertain world.

It is impossible to know whether the Europeans of the early renaissance intended to create a sense of permanence by producing the art and architecture they did on such a grand scale. To stand in the beating heart of Florence and gaze up at the Baptistry in the Piazza Duomo with its monumental bronze doors, it seems as if it were built to last forever. But we can surmise a few things about Florentine intentions by looking at their world.

First of all, in the decay of the Roman Empire, they saw a handmade empire in ruins. They saw an all-powerful Church bloated and corrupt, with popes who openly delighted in prostitutes and sold indulgences.

They saw a natural world that was a threshold to creative inspiration and a spiritual connection to God, and that held the raw material for manifesting their own dreams.

The RenGen aesthetic is a similar concoction. It accepts imperfection but punishes flawed intentions. It revels in an infusion of sights, sounds, ideas, and visions that have the same effect as a collage. In fact, collage theory, it turns out, also applies to the RenGen aesthetic.

The Big Picture Is a Collage

From where I stood looking out of a thirty-second-story window, Millennium Park in Chicago looked like a colossal, animated collage. There is video art projected on a fountain where children skip and splash each other, an oversized silver bean sculpture where lovers rendezvous, and a grassy apron where picnickers spread out in front of the Frank Gehry–designed band shell with its muscular steel ribbon that sits atop it like the gift box the bean sculpture came in. I think back on what Tony Jones from the School of the Art Institute told me: "Collage is the defining art form of the twenty-first century." Of course it is, and, in fact, collage is a visual metaphor for the RenGen. It captures the soul of the RenGen aesthetic. Collage is unpretentious, collaborative, interdisciplinary, and flexible enough to be cocreated. It is cross-disciplinary, imperfect, impermanent, irregular, endlessly renewable, and recyclable. The RenGen steps out every day into a gigantic visual and aural collage called life.

Everything that can be produced must first be designed. The energy being generated by all the artistic output described elsewhere in the book triggers the RenGen aesthetic. Naturally, when the people who train as artists or aspire to a creative life become active consumers, we can expect that they'll want a certain look and feel to the things that surround them. But the artists and designers I encountered want to make more than something fetching to look at, they want to make meaning. As the problems of the society grow more complex—grinding poverty, global warming, overcrowding, and limited natural resources—these artists, professionally trained or amateur, will help bridge to the next civilization with the force of their creative energy.

CHAPTER SEVEN

Youth Culture

The burning question for many professional people, from marketers to teachers, is how to reach the next generation of influencers. The road to the Boomers is well worn and easy to navigate. However, the road that leads to the youth segment of today's population is a winding two-track marked with potholes. Once there, social norms shift like the weather, and the people speak in cultural codes difficult for outsiders to translate. These young people were born into a world of hyperconnectivity, and signs are everywhere that this generation thinks and learns very differently from their forebears. They are fully digital and maintain vast networks of acquaintances in multiple countries via the Internet. Just like the Boomers, however, the things they gravitate toward will change the way we all do things. Certainly, their role in the RenGen will be decisive for our civilization.

Today's young people will inherit a complex world with daunting challenges—an unstable global economy, social sectarianism, and an endangered ecosystem, just to name a few. "To meet the challenges that we now face as a nation, we all must recognize the voices of our young people; we must understand their challenges and needs. We must in earnest research youth culture," believes Carl Taylor, professor of education and a youth culture expert at Michigan State University and blogger on youth culture.

Taking up that challenge, I set out with my research team to discover the motivations of this emerging generation, in order to predict their role as the RenGen. People as diverse as marketers, game developers, educators, and librarians provided their insights. We looked at young people's interests in music, visual art, and fashion. Our team looked at the range of creative expression youth show an interest in—from garage bands to graffiti art, hip-hop to the ubiquitous MySpace.com, graphic novels to cell-phone video art; there was plenty of cultural material from which to choose. So rich, in fact, was the range of young people's activity that it demanded a focus.

In the end, I found the most telling patterns were reflected in two very different areas: poetry and online multiplayer games. It's a situation that harkens back to John Naisbett's popular book *Megatrends*, where he predicted that hi-tech and hi-touch would walk hand-in-hand to create balance between the useful but dehumanizing isolation that is technology and people's need to for intimacy.

The Digital Mind

I spent the better part of a year looking for the perfect expert to explain to me what the big deal is about online multiplayer games. Most people wanted to talk about the size of the market, which is gigantic—players of the game WarCraft form a larger population than the city of Chicago—or the money to be made, $9.3 billion, as of this writing—more money than Hollywood box office movies in America ($8.8 billion in 2005). And as more and more games go online, the global gaming industry is expected to soon outpace the sales of both the record industry and of home video rentals within the United States! However, I wanted to know what lived beneath the surface of the numbers. Why was this all so compelling an experience for these players, most of whom were between the ages of 10 and 18? And what does the persistence of its popularity portend for the future? Then, at a professional conference, the expert found me.

I had time to kill between meetings, so I glanced at the list of the day's speakers and was attracted to a panel on the Internet and new learning models. If I hustled I could make it. The room was quite dark when I entered, with only the glow from the PowerPoint® projection. When my eyes adjusted there was Professor Constance Steinkuhler at the podium. Blond and statuesque, she was dressed in a fashionable outfit that gave her an air of worldliness.

If you are like me, multiplayer online games are not an everyday entertainment. I did manage to get a firsthand glimpse from my 17-year-old son, who agreed to tour me through one of the most popular games. I soon discovered that, as Elizabeth Kolbert wrote in the *New Yorker* in 2001, these games are "persistent social and material worlds, loosely structured by open-ended (fantasy) narratives, where players are largely free to do as they please—slay ogres, siege castles, barter goods in town, or shake the fruit out of the trees. They are notorious for their peculiar combination of designed 'escapist fantasy' yet emergent 'social realism.'"

To interact in these games, a player takes on a digital persona known as an avatar; this is a character that you can personalize by giving it specific features including a name. Your avatar becomes an extension of you and interacts with others in the multiplayer game world. The term *avatar* itself is borrowed from ancient mythology, where it refers to an advanced initiate who incarnates the divine.

For two years, Professor Steinkuhler, an educational technology expert from the University of Wisconsin, Madison, studied the online, multiplayer game world. Her analysis is drawn from following a group of 22 persistent players over a two-year period, managing an online "guild" of more than 160 loyal players, as well as sampling and tracking similarities in game design across a spectrum of games. From this process Steinkuhler made some important discoveries.

The gaming environment demands high levels of literacy. Since all communications are written and read, online gamers generate page upon page of text over hours of play. The make-believe world of multiplayer games is also rich in storytelling and character development. These are the same qualities we look for in good literature. Consider the following exchange between Steinkuhler and one of her online subjects.

Liadon and I are hunting together on our elven avatars. His is over level 40, mine is quite new and barely level 15. We are in the Elven Forest, talking idly in the party chat channel while hunting together, so that I might have practice playing an elf.

Liadon: you know how the fairies originally came into being, right?
Adeliede: no how?

Liadon: Oooh, story time! once, back when the world was young and the gods roamed the world as mortals, Einhasad was in the forest and decided to create the race of elves. none of the other creatures wanted to help because they did not know it was Einhasad in her mortal form

Adeliede: oh!

Liadon: But 4 exceptionally kind creatures did give their assistance. that is another story entirely, but one was the humble butterfly. She did not have much to offer, but spared some dust from her wings to allow Einhasad to make the elves. As a reward, those butterflies who assisted were given the gift of immortality and made fairies. The fairy queen was the original butterfly

Adeliede: how did u know all that?

Liadon: I'm smart :p *[joking face]* Every elf knows that. Seriously, though. the mother tree told me.

Such games are a vehicle for self-expression. Players design their avatar personas and create much of the detail of the game's setting. There are, for instance, guild and fan Web sites that feature original works that players create based on the virtual worlds they inhabit. Players post art, poetry, and short stories.

Behaviors and Attitudes from the Digital Mind

This desire to contribute creative content shows no signs of waning. Theoretically, a broader interpretive process is underway as players define the virtual world to make meaning. "Like all interpretive communities," Steinkuhler explains, "they take up the symbolic, cultural materials offered [to] them by [the] media to collectively create the form and substance of their own cultural worlds. In this way, they are no different from the cultures of old, except that, now, the consumers have increasingly user-friendly tools at their disposal to work with, including online access to socio-technical networks that enable their easy distribution."

Creative Play

The very content of the games is self-generating. This means the users shape the nature of the content by interacting with it. R.G. Collingwood, author of the seminal book *The Principles of Art*, determined that mass art is often the most passive. The interactive nature of video games, then, marks an important cultural development. By contrast, video games are possibly the first "cocreative" mechanically reproduced form of art: they are mass artworks shaped by audience input. Interactivity is a crucial distinction between more passive mass art forms such as film, novels, and recorded music and new interactive mass art forms. Video game players are anything but mentally or intellectually passive during typical game play.

As a consequence, the make-believe worlds of the games are a platform for all kinds of creative output. For instance, Steinkuhler found that school-aged kids are perfectly willing to engage in long, thoughtful creative writing projects written from the perspective of their avatar identities. In fact, she found several of her subjects took on thoughtful writing projects in their spare time, not as an isolated "assignment" but as part and parcel of what it means to game online. She asked one of the gamers if he planned to show his short story to his teacher at school. "No way," he answered with a hint of contempt. This suggests that although online gaming is hugely popular, the literary aspect of it is relatively hidden from the education community.

A Collaborative Work Ethic

Most successful gamers are collaborative. In fact, they learn collaboratively. However, this is not how the games were designed originally. Steinkuhler tells me that early on, all online games incorporated the standard "kill monsters, gain riches, get better equipment in order to kill monsters more efficiently" cycle. But in the popular game Lineage II, that "treadmill is notably slower, more laborious, and, well, painful." It is a setting that, by design, tends to favor social collaboration over flat-out grinding through levels of slaying and leaping.

It is no wonder, then, that notions such as "social interdependence" and "group efficiency" play an important role in the way that many gamers engage with Lineage. Socially interdependent gamers are repeatedly described as more outgoing, willing "to talk to anyone out of the blue." As one participant aptly described the difference in one of Steinkuhler's studies: "The third one would be running off and killing stuff, while the other two would be standing there talking to each other about how to help each other level up."

To listen to Steinkuhler's stories from the two years she spent living virtually in the massive multiplayer gaming community, the picture that emerges is one of inhabitants who are creative, self-expressive, and networked within communities with reciprocal systems of support. She describes it as an expansive community of online players, all of whom share a lore and a language that help participants create a sense of belonging and meaning.

"Now imagine it populated with others from across the globe who gather in virtual inns and taverns, gossiping about the most popular guild or comparing notes on the best hunting spots," Steinkuhler writes. "Imagine yourself in a heated battle for the local castle, with live opponents from all over collaborating or competing with you. Imagine a place where you can be the brave hero, the kingdom rogue, or the village sage, developing a reputation for yourself that is known from Peoria to Peking. Now imagine that you could come from school or work, drop your book bag on the ground, log in, and enter that world any day, any time, anywhere."

The multiplayer online game world turns out to be a rambling endlessly self-evocative playground for collaborative young creatives. It is yielding a student, soon-to-become worker, whose ethics and imagination have been formatted by this digital realm. People in business and education have much to learn from the work of people like Steinkuhler. She has taken the time to understand the deeper satisfactions available to youth in creative digital worlds, as they design new identities and forge clans that give their make-believe world a rich, personal meaning.

The Live Poets Society:
Hi-touch Counterpoint to a High-tech Society

While online games are massively popular among the common youth culture, there is another side to the coin. It is the low-tech, organically grown phenomenon of poetry. In particular, poetry slams. The poetry slam format got its start in Chicago in the 1980s. From its humble beginnings as a contest between two dueling poets at an open mike night, it grew into an international movement. Here is a description of one of the early venues for poetry slamming from an article by K. Heinz that gives you a sense of how far it has come:

As an actual venue, The Get Me High Lounge was a small, damp, run-down bar set in the very center of Chicago's Bucktown neighborhood. The walls were narrow, painted black and graffiti'd upon, as though they were a chalkboard. News clippings, album covers, and old jazz posters smothered what was left of the walls. . . . The club survived on late night jazz performances most of the week under Butchie's proprietorship. Butchie spoke only a minimal, rapidly muttered English to his new guests, if he spoke much at all, though he did heckle the poets. The clientele often felt they'd arrived into another anxious, dangerous but enticing world.

The current generation of young poets took the poetry slam into the mainstream. Today, the International Youth Poetry Slam attracts the participation of more than 5,000 people from as far away as the Ukraine. Benjamin Ortiz, a young poetry enthusiast, describes the event this way: "I saw 45 teams of four poets each of who slammed their way out of regular local series all over the country in order to qualify to converge in Texas. I saw 1,200 people pack the Paramount Theater. I saw CNN and NPR following wordsmiths from the Nuyorican Poets Club, which sends a brand new team of rookies every year to nationals, winning the championship that year and propelling once-unknown bards into national stardom. I saw the light."

Poetry slamming exploded when it snuggled up to hip-hop. Entrepreneur and producer Russell Simmons created a Broadway review, Def Poetry Jam, based solely on the performances of young poets who took turns upping the emotional ante with their poignant and dramatic poems. The *New York Times* theater critic gave it a glowing review and Simmons took the show on tour.

Poetry is the literary genre of choice for youth. They incorporate poems into their college entrance applications, their online face pages, and, like the poets of the first renaissance, they write love poems to their sweethearts. The poetry scene has caught on in towns big and small. On a spring night in my small town of 40,000 residents that lies due west of Chicago, the local library hosted a youth poetry contest. Winners would be decided by applause. "How many people showed up?" I asked my son. It was packed, he told me. Later, the librarian who organized the event told me they expected twenty and got more like a hundred.

Looking Forward:
Practical Implications of Youth Culture

What do the interests and expressions of this young segment of the RenGen portend for the future? I think there are a few possibilities. The first is that this generation will usher in a new way of teaching and learning. While parents worry that too much time spent in front of the PC might cripple their children socially and intellectually, the research tells a different story. These environments teach potent lessons and build hard skills like reading and writing. They are also illustrative in ways a straight lecture can't be. Chris Dede, a professor at the Harvard Graduate School of Education, believes learning and entertainment environments will converge and be delivered on portable wireless devices that will infuse our daily lives. Dede researches online learning models and predicts kids will learn through "augmented reality, where smart objects interact within intelligent contexts" to help teach middle and high schoolers about science and society.

The way we teach and the way we learn have consequences in everyday life. A new way of teaching and learning will have implications for management when this segment enters the work force. It also affects how new products with sharp learning curves get introduced. Our current educational system lags far behind the capacity of the young minds of the RenGen, but as the wider culture fills in with new instructional models, progress continues regardless.

Second, this generation has a "we are one world" xenophile's appreciation for many cultures. "It no longer matters whether you live in upper Manhattan, the Upper Peninsula of Michigan, or in the middle of a small fishing village in Alaska, youth are no longer isolated because of locale," asserts professor Carl Taylor of Michigan State University. This implies growing tolerance of cultural differences and a belief in a fair voice for all.

Que Gaskins, vice president of lifestyle and entertainment marketing at Reebok agrees. He notes, "It is very important to help teens celebrate their individuality, and accept it in others. They openly share their religion, ethnicity, and what makes them unique." The case for tolerance among creative types has been eloquently made by such authors as Richard Florida. But tolerance often suggests the need to put up with differences, or at least look the other way. The point to be made here is that today's young creative types groove on variety, choice, and the freedom to align themselves among the broadest array of cohorts.

Why?

Because for this segment of the RenGen, diversity signals strength. They live in a collaborative world defined by interdependence and cooperation, and this age group has learned important social lessons about the benefits of surrounding themselves with people who are different from themselves. There is plenty of room to be optimistic about an age group when their motivation to embrace diversity is spurred by goodwill and good sense.

One final point remains. This younger age group in the Ren-Gen favors a meritocracy. Expect them to align themselves with peers, politicians, role models, and bosses who get things done. They will be less swayed by pedigree or credentials, and they will allow interlopers to lead—provided they have a bold vision and a track record of achievement. As such, they will define success on different terms. Rather than buckle under the weight of the social, political, and economic climate they inherit, they will measure perseverance itself as an achievement. Joining forces to achieve a greater result will also be characteristic of their progress, as will a balance between individual ego needs and the good of the group.

Despite their pragmatism, they will not give up happiness and personal freedoms. They differ from realists in that, as Albert Camus said, "Realists only undertake jobs that will succeed, therefore, they never undertake anything that is truly important or humane." I emerge from my research on this group with confidence in what lies ahead for them. By and large, they will create meaning based on hope, effort, and humanity.

CHAPTER EIGHT

RenGen Spirituality

To take the full measure of the RenGen mind-set, we need to explore how this group is pursuing spiritual enlightenment in the age of rebirth. Earlier, we discussed the work of Pitirim Sorokin, whose exhaustive survey of the life cycles of civilizations led him to conclude that as one civilization declines, another emerges. Moreover, as this shift occurs, there is a point of synthesis between the culture heading for demise and the one that is about to be born.

When the beliefs that organized the declining civilization no longer serve to help people adapt to their world—for instance, by organizing them to build communities, or by dispensing moral guidelines, or by providing solace in the midst of life's hardships—then one of three things happens for the people in that period:

- Some people cease embracing those beliefs.
- Some people cling to them fervently.
- And some combine that portion of those beliefs that are still meaningful with new truths, thereby giving rise to a new belief system.

The spiritual life of the RenGen exists at this juncture. To some, it is a call to preserve old beliefs, while others have gathered around a spiritual order that is a mélange of practices and beliefs derived from long-established faiths. Still others have mentally packed up and set off on a journey to discover what their beliefs should be.

The Conversion from Religion to Spirituality

Americans are still largely Christian—between 75 and 85 percent are Protestant or Catholic. So, what has changed? According to a recent Gallup poll, there is a growing trend toward personal fulfillment and individual experience of the divine. More and more Americans are fusing the faiths of their upbringings with explorations into other ways of approaching God and nature through more mystical methods. Others are disaffected or infrequent Christians, or people who have turned away from traditional approaches entirely in their search for a new path to transcendence. What we are experiencing is the messy process of building a new belief system.

The rise of the self-help movement paved the way for a transformation. This movement has been gathering followers of all stripes since the 1970s, when individuals began to disengage from the institutions, particularly religious, that had disillusioned them. Many turned within and sought to teach themselves.

As a consequence of this self-reliance, people have an increasing need to anchor spirituality in secular situations, such as their domestic life or work environments. Designated places in the home for prayer and contemplation are increasingly common.

According to a poll by *House & Garden* magazine, 82 percent of people consider a quiet, meditative space the most necessary part of their home.

People have begun to talk about their work lives as their "purpose" or "calling." Many buy books on meditation and daily intentions to put themselves in charge of accessing the divine, without the help of minister, rabbi, or priest. When going it alone proves either disappointing or isolating, people seek help from mediums, life coaches, motivational books, career planning, and other forms of assisted self-help. To the extent that people have searched for a path to transcendence through internal reflection, they have also sought external support to make the journey more focused.

The Entrepreneurial Clerics of the RenGen

I am seated across the dinner table from Jennifer A. She has laid out a meal of wild-caught salmon and a colorful array of vegetables from her garden. A sumptuous-looking homemade cake awaits on the sideboard. We are meeting to discuss Jennifer's next steps with her career. "I need to make some choices about which angle to pursue in my profession," she confides. "I'm stuck. I need to get to the next level." Jennifer is a RenGen cleric. Having devoted countless hours to training in yoga, reiki massage therapy, medicinal flower essences, akashic records interpretation, meditation practices, and more, Jennifer has invested more time and money on her education than the average Ph.D.

Jennifer's trouble is that the new spiritualism in America has a rubber ceiling—there is no clear path to upward mobility. There is no hierarchy with ranks to rise through. It is a laissez-faire marketplace that bestows influence on figures like Wayne Dyer and Deepak Chopra, who also happen to be talented entrepreneurs. With no credentialing body, it's a religious Wild West. Despite this, Jennifer has a thriving practice with clients from all walks of life who seek her healing therapies. The quandary she faces now is emblematic of the struggle for credibility that hinders the new belief system from taking root faster. Without an organized system allowing RenGen clerics to gain credibility in the marketplace, total conversion of people toward more mystical practices will be attained by the few, not the many. However, enough of these practices are so intriguing to large numbers of seekers who cherry-pick practices like yoga and meditation to adopt.

Like much of the RenGen culture, spiritual life is a fusion of contemporary beliefs and personal explorations, combined with old-fashioned religious traditions. While there is a discernible rise in spirituality, it's also true that America's religiosity has been a constant factor in the American belief system over the last seventy-five years, and more than 85 percent of Americans continue to identify themselves with one of the major faiths. What *has* eroded is Americans' confidence that religion has a meaningful influence on public life.

Still, Americans' sense of the importance of faith in their personal lives has held steady and even grown. As RenGenners retain spiritual beliefs from the religions of their mothers and fathers, newly adopted spiritual practices will continue to fuse with more conventional religious writing and practices. Consider the case of Marianne Williamson, who has made a career out of her lifelong study of the weighty mystical text *A Course in Miracles*. Her remarkable success has a great deal to do with her ability to address many popular concerns using a religious tone, but without rattling the orthodoxies too much. Her books are bestsellers among the RenGen searching for new beliefs and not wanting to abandon old traditions.

The Exaltation of Roots

The religious traditions that endure are those that rest most snugly against a person's roots. Religious rituals move us because they claim a special relationship to the milestones in our lives—marriages, births, deaths, and so on. They also touch our deepest yearnings, which include the following.

A need for security

Given the relative prosperity of much of RenGen society, security needs are rarely as basic as food, clothing, and shelter. Rather, the RenGen savor the freedom to search out their spiritual identities and make personal connections to a greater power. But the price of this self-reliance is fear—fear that you have made the wrong choices, fear that you are using the wrong method of prayer, fear that you have identified with the wrong religious community, and, in the end, fear that you are utterly lost about who you are and what you want out of life.

This is a heavy burden that the rituals of traditional religion cannot lighten, as they emphasize a reinforcement of the tenets of the faith rather than an exploration of the soul. What traditional religion does offer is the comfort of recognition that comes from an established and collectively understood meaning of life. Therefore, the RenGen understand existential loneliness, but they still seek comfort in the security of the familiar traditions of worship. For instance, a Jewish couple may celebrate the high holidays with their families and at the same time practice an Eastern style of meditation. A Catholic woman may accept Christ as her savior, but also believe in reincarnation.

A sense of belonging

Connection to community is a growing obsession for the RenGen. The success of organic food clubs, book clubs, and peer-coaching organizations bear witness to the power of community. Rick Warren's colossal bestseller, *The Purpose-Driven Life*, succeeded, in part, because it provided more than 400,000 ministers in 162 countries a recipe for gathering seekers for weekly reading and discussion groups. Warren's definition of the meaning of life revolves around evangelism, worship, ministry, discipleship, and fellowship. He taps into people's need to belong to a group that respects them not for their material success, but for doing good works and being better people. This ideology represents a maturing of the self-help movement.

For many, Warren's point of view grants permission for people to like themselves even if they haven't achieved the big goals they set, or even if the lifestyle changes they made haven't delivered the desired result. The plain truth of the matter is that, even after a steady dose of self-help doctrine, many people have awakened and found themselves still selling life insurance or teaching school. They aren't living like millionaires with a beach house in Hawaii, as motivational guru Tony Robbins had inspired them to attain. Rather, by subscribing to the philosophy of *The Purpose-Driven Life*, they've found that their lives still have meaning, regardless of their status or wealth.

The RenGen live in a culture that is beginning to turn away from materialism and move toward more transcendent visions. Rick Warren's book resonates with regular people caught on the cusp of that shift—people who find it uplifting to join with other seekers to synthesize these principles into a new moral basis for everyday life.

A quest for transcendence

The RenGen aspire to reach a higher level of consciousness through union of body, mind, and spirit, one in which communication with the divine is attained by training the consciousness to open itself to divinely channeled information. A practice that is easier said than done. This spirituality emphasizes the value of meditation, which has its roots in Eastern religions. Sam Harris, the author of *The End of Faith*, has a thesis on the difference between Eastern and Western spirituality that can be boiled down to this: For Christian, Jewish, and Muslim faiths, the emphasis is on the faith itself. This has little to do with the nature of transcendence. Consciousness is defined as the sum total of our thoughts, perceptions, sensations, and feelings.

In a heightened state, our consciousness allows for divine enlightenment. Some form of meditation is generally believed to be an effective path to attaining this enlightenment. The trouble is, with or without an instruction manual, meditation is a murky practice without easily quantifiable or measurable results.

If people seek a road map into their consciousness, they eventually find themselves looking to the Eastern practices of Buddhists, for example, who have developed sophisticated spiritual instructions for training the mind to access consciousness. To put the new belief system more within reach, the RenGen are seeking out ancient texts. The Bible, the works of St. Augustine, and Shambhala Buddhist translations are all the focus of renewed interest. RenGenners are also increasingly curious about the lives of the spiritually gifted, such as saints and mystics who model the individual's journey toward God both within and outside the structures of organized faith.

Rise of the Cling-ons

Not everyone is fusing the old with the new. For some, the bedrock of their reality is based on beliefs born of traditional religion. It is in the religious and spiritual sensibilities of the RenGen that we find some of the most overt examples of social polarization. As the old beliefs erode, there are those who react by clinging to their cherished beliefs. Prime among these beliefs is that one's chosen faith grants eternal life. A 2002 Pew Research Center study revealed that nearly *one in five* Americans believe that theirs is the one true faith assuring eternal life. Indeed, these believers are making their voices heard out of proportion to their numbers, especially on issues like the teaching of creationism versus evolution and the legalization of same-sex marriage. According to the study, "They are joined by the less strictly devout, who still see a symbolic role for established belief in American life (for instance, according to Gallup, three-quarters of Americans favor the passage of an amendment permitting voluntary prayer in schools)." Guarding the symbols of a belief system can be construed as an attempt to forestall the decline of the overall civilization.

I dub this group the Cling-ons because they clutch their traditional beliefs with a ferocity that is warlike. They leave no doubt that they seek to dominate. Still, this group serves a useful purpose, staking out points of view that broaden the middle ground for the majority to develop new perspectives on faith. Also, until the RenGen gather enough momentum to define their beliefs, the Cling-ons represent the library of traditions from which the new belief system will borrow its canon. They are every bit as important to the rebirth as those people who subject themselves to the tortured introspection that accompanies the search for a new belief system. (Appropriately, many such seekers actually call this process as "the work.") For now, the groups coexist, albeit tenuously.

So, we have a series of contradictions afloat in a roiling sea of possibilities. Even as many Americans reject the well-trodden paths to God, still others fill mega-churches led by celebrity ministers. This obscures the simple truth uniting all seekers, whatever their religious or spiritual persuasion: Now, more than ever, people feel the need for a spiritual practice that connects them to a source of enlightenment. This enlightenment occurs in the private exchange between the seeker and the divine. The implication is that only evidence that the enlightenment can be achieved is through self-report, not through ceremonial rites of passage.

As more people take this journey, they draw comfort from the reports of other seekers. This is a form of teaching and learning that, strikingly, brings us full circle back to humanism—the belief in the ability of ordinary men and women to discover truths by themselves and as a community.

It will take time for us to see which tenets of the emerging belief system will stick. Christianity had the benefit of a book and a savior in human form to attract followers. If the RenGen represent the beginnings of a new belief system based on a spiritual consciousness, then that is an ambiguous proposition. What is called for, along with prayer and meditation, is imagination, which this generation has in abundance. Whatever the process, or however long it takes to evolve, a new belief system will eventually arise and achieve critical mass.

CHAPTER NINE

The Collaborative Context— How The RenGen Gets Things Done

Earlier in my career, I worked for an educational film company. I was assigned to work on a training video about how to hire good people. No, not just good people, the "best" people. The subtext of the script held a dirty little secret that went something like this: Team players are losers. Why? Because team players are followers, not leaders. The "teamwork" model that the training video was addressing was primarily a management-driven, top-down relic of the industrial age. By contrast, collaboration is how things will get done in a RenGen.

But, as we will see in this chapter, collaborating in a knowledge economy is a different affair. The period of decline right before a renaissance sets up an imperative that galvanizes people. Collaboration becomes essential for organizing people and pooling their ideas, expertise, and information. Consider the gravity of the problems facing the RenGen, the technocracy in which we work, and people's increasing drive to be creative—these aspects all demand a new work style that favors collaborative, not top-down, management.

High Stakes—Deep Purpose

At the core of every problem is a sense of purpose. If the period right before a renaissance is marked by decline and decay, we can expect there is quite a lot of practical work to be done. Add to that a catastrophic event that hastens the collapse of the declining civilization, and you have motivation of heroic proportions. This inspires people. When teams organize around projects where the stakes are high—people are in danger of dying, or a 40-block area of a city has been wiped out, or the polar ice caps are melting— many of the turf issues that might otherwise make teamwork difficult are set aside as the group bonds toward a higher purpose.

It should be cause for optimism that as a civilization nears the point of rebirth, there is often a simultaneous growth spurt of talented, creative people who come to the fore. Many of them work as freelancers, as they have mastered certain specialties that allow them to compete for work and survive in their niches. However, these niches are codependent with other niches to create a final product. We can expect that the circumstances of the RenGen call for work on high-stakes problems in high-concept ways—and that this will draw these diverse specialists together.

The Specialist Versus the Generalist

A debate is underway about whether specialists or generalists are better suited to resolve the most deep-seated problems of our times. Our traditional idea of a "renaissance" person is someone who has a breadth of knowledge. Although that quality remains true for the RenGen, mainly because we know that creative people have a large storehouse of knowledge from which to PING against, the reality is that we live in a technocracy that has fostered specialized knowledge in all disciplines. This fact dictates that more people will be required to collaborate to pool information and ideas across specialties.

Learning to lead as well as to follow

How do collaborative teams avoid the inertia wrought by too many opinions or the reductive compromise of consensus? The examples of successful collaboration my team looked at—many of them from the arts, education, and technology sectors—showed a style where individuals take the lead on issues where they have expertise and follow in other circumstances. The more experienced the teams and the more self-confident the members, the more graceful the handoff of leadership tends to be. Harvey Seifter, author of the book *Leadership Ensemble*, was formerly the executive director of the Orpheus Chamber Orchestra, an orchestra unique in its lack of a conductor. It relied solely on a collaborative model.

Seifter points out the empowering aspect of the process when team members feel in control of tough situations: "It's the musicians who figure out how to adapt Friday night's successful performance in a 400-seat hall in Easton, Pennsylvania, to the special needs of Carnegie Hall . . . and implement the changes in an hour or two on Saturday morning." But Seifter goes on to note that in high-stakes situations, the symphony knew and respected specialties and often invited the "expert" to step forward.

Sociability

Now more than ever, sociability matters in collaborative situations. By sociability, I mean a personal disposition toward interacting with one's colleagues with a sense of openness, good-will, and empathy. At Pixar Studios, sociability ranks among the two most important skills the company values in an employee. The first is an ability to communicate visually (drawings, sketches, animations, models) in what are group situations. Pixar defines sociability as someone who can sit in a "concepting" session and allow fellow team members to draw on his work without taking umbrage. On the flip side, it is considered uncool to use such sessions for paybacks of any kind through idea assassination. This suggests that part of sociability is a sensitivity to the tacit rules for interaction that keep people setting collectively high standards while still remaining helpful to one another.

For the RenGen, the vastness of the Internet enables collaboration among endless combinations of people. Interactions, even by e-mail, are always social because they require that we engage with other people, different cultures, and communities of practice, or with the cultural tools (disciplinary languages, methodologies, and customs) created and used by those specialties. No matter what the focus of the team, people adept at the give-and-take have more currency than those with extraordinary skills who lack the personality traits that enable teams to create great work under pressure.

Talent Attracts Talent

We can take some lessons from the way in which Michelangelo managed some very talented collaborators. First of all, a determined, visionary master must "own" the project. This quality of person naturally attracts attention to the project, allowing him to recruit critical talent in the early phases. These coworkers/ collaborators are people who seek the challenge, notoriety, and legacy such an experience bestows. They will also make their way through the stormy moods that swirl around a high-stakes project, as they were attracted by the associated thrill of working with a master on a grand scale in the first place. They are thus willing to suffer unpleasantness in exchange for interacting with brilliance. Their tolerance for struggle also has to do in some measure with their sociability. Creative people describe feelings of profound gratification from working in teams of highly talented people that supersedes any individual ego needs.

Finally, the most talented people tend to enjoy higher levels of difficulty—period. As we discussed in Chapter 4 on the creative personality, people of this ilk tend to have an inner drive. They sink long hours of grueling effort into a project without complaint if it gives them the right opportunities for expressing their talents.

The Learning Continuum of Collaboration

One related issue needs to be addressed. People who engage in collaborative work do better when they commit to learning throughout. In this case, learning means the construction of knowledge. In the settings I am describing, team members come with individual reservoirs of knowledge, but then they also have to be active participants in learning collectively. Much of what they learn comes from their interactions with others. This is one of the ways collaboration differs from industrial-model teamwork. The latter involves a division of labor interwoven with some brainstorming. Collaboration involves give and take, an interweaving of teaching and learning that intensifies the effort.

This style of learning points up the situational nature of collaboration. Think of it this way: in most settings, work-related learning occurs within specific departments or disciplines. We work with colleagues, attend professional conferences together, and read and swap articles in our field of endeavor. When cross-disciplinary teams are gathered to tackle complex projects, learning is influenced by that enlarged context. Questions become more expansive. Members of the team serve as ambassadors for their way of thinking, expressed through practices, customs, and jargon. Minds are changed. The situation demands that people understand and put to use theories and methods from disciplines other than their own. So learning remains a constant. It's no surprise, then, that some players are exhilarated by the mental effort demanded by collaboration while others are exhausted by it.

The RenGen will develop practices around ways of working collaboratively. Collaboration is necessary in a renaissance for a variety of reasons—primarily that big solutions and innovative ideas are born from diverse knowledge and expertise. The trouble is that the act of collaborating is its own skill. Part of the RenGen task is to turn collaboration into a discipline. They will need to address the interplay between the substance and the procedure of the collaborative process to help people gracefully take on projects of grander vision. Those who do will have attained a precious skill in what is the new currency of the work world. They will be one of the "best" people to hire.

CHAPTER TEN

The RenGen Company

Organizations looking to market to the cultural consumer need not get into the business of producing or exhibiting creative work, although companies like Starbucks and BMW are doing so. Some companies will want to consider a more traditional role, like that of the Renaissance-era Medicis who sponsored art competitions and outdoor festivals to stimulate the market as well as to earn loyalty and respect among the people of Florence.

In the United States, corporate sponsorship of arts and culture represents only 5 percent of overall sponsorship spending. Yet, a panel of *New Yorker* subscribers drawn from across the country noticed and valued corporations who supported the arts. Furthermore, they are more likely than the general public to buy from businesses that support the arts.

In 1997, the Performance Research Group, a company that measures a sponsor's return on investment, surveyed arts patrons across a spectrum of offerings including museums, symphonies, opera, dance, and theater, and noted that 44 percent of arts patrons they surveyed held more trust in companies that sponsor cultural events—compared to only 17 percent of U.S. Olympic audiences. Yet, according to the International Events Group, 67 percent of all sponsorship spending in 2006 went to sporting events.

This inequity has a couple of explanations. First, there is the matter of adapting to the unknown. In our survey of 1,400 marketing executives (discussed in Appendix C), they told us that two of their most desired targets—affluents and women—would best be reached through marketing tied to arts and entertainment. The problem was, they were not as certain about how to execute such a strategy. In fact, one quarter (24.5%) responded that they would be most interested in learning more about arts and entertainment marketing.

Another barrier is that corporations have traditionally had more of a comfort level with sponsoring sports over the arts. For example, I once had a young vice president at a major international consulting firm tell me that the Yo-Yo Ma concert he sponsored had delivered new business, along with a generous amount of media attention in his local market. But it was still a risky move for him internally; there were lots of questions from management. He got no such scrutiny when sponsoring a golf tournament. "Guys walk out into the hallway carrying their putters and slap me on the back."

There is another hidden factor to consider that has kept companies from embracing the cultural consumer. Business is an inherently competitive activity. It makes a company look more competitive if it aligns itself with a competitive activity such as professional sports. Businesses should never lose sight of what it takes to be competitive. But the fact of the matter is that "what it takes" to be competitive is up for revision. It's not so much an either/or, but for savvy marketers, it is "and also" that brings their marketing portfolios into balance. Progressive companies will look to diversify their investments in marketing to reflect a more RenGen strategy by redistributing some of the 67 percent of status quo spending on sports marketing.

Collaboration Is the New Model

Current economic trends point to a worldwide economy that is slowly recovering from a turbulent economic start to the twenty-first century. This backdrop of economic deceleration has led to an awareness that collaboration is a necessary—not a "might be nice"—business practice. A white paper authored by Cap Gemini, a worldwide consulting practice, puts it this way: "Collaborative working is perhaps the single most important factor in achieving competitive advantage and long-term success for organizations." As competition for resources and talent heightens worldwide, we will continue to see less emphasis placed on centralized decision making—situations where the coach calls the plays and they get handed down to the team from the top—in favor of collaborative cohorts, groups of talented specialists who perform as an ensemble. In this situation, cultural marketing serves to strengthen a company's image as a strong collaborator.

A few intrepid marketers have found a way to wade in without losing their footing. In the arena of live theater, Visa, General Motors, and Anheuser Busch to cite a few notable examples, have stayed true to their overall marketing posture and gone big. They have made promotional alliances with Broadway producers, and in the case of GM, bought naming rights to theatrical houses.

Financial services companies staked out their campgrounds: theater, symphonies, performing arts, and museums—and their target is the VIVIDs. American Express, like other pioneers of this trend, has developed highly sophisticated strategies for sponsoring things like historical preservation of international monuments, for which the company invested $10 million and used the commitment to communicate to cultural tourists through tying in with their travel services and credit cards.

PNC Bank has a successful relationship in Philadelphia with the renowned Philadelphia Flower Show, something they use whenever possible as a collaborative vehicle for copromotions of the Philadelphia Museum, Franklin Museum, and Philly Fun Guide—all cultural entertainment partners who benefit from PNC support.

Does it work? Regina Harger, a vice president at PNC Bank explains, "Our philosophy is one of 'enlightened self-interest.' We feel strongly that arts and culture are economic drivers of the region, and when the region does well the bank does well." But she goes on to explain that everyone at the bank, from the CEO on down, embraces the strategy of working with arts and entertainment in the region, primarily because it helps them engage with their customers over events that have meaning for the customer.

Harger spoke of the account managers in their financial services department who enjoy placing the calls to their high–net worth customers to invite them to a preview of the flower show or a private tour of a blockbuster art exhibition that is sold out. "This delivers value to our most important bottom line: relationships."

An Aesthetic for Everyone

While this approach is not particularly new, what *is* new is how broadly and quickly it will expand as the RenGen aesthetic heats up. What was a niche interest will look more mass market. Companies that lack a distinctive style or message that makes associations with that aesthetic will start to falter.

Indeed, even a warhorse like Boeing has begun to see the allure of the RenGen aesthetic. The company explored it through its philanthropic support of events like live theater and Latin jazz concerts. Boeing's Jim Newcomb explains, "Our exit surveys told us that people felt two things about our sponsorship: one, they felt recognized—that their community was being acknowledged for having a concert series worthy of such support. The other thing they felt was gratitude." Newcomb did everything he could to communicate those feelings internally to Boeing employees.

The result was powerful.

He explained that it gave employees a sense of social "currency." Not surprisingly, Newcomb was moved up and over into brand management to become Senior Manager of Corporate Identity and Sponsorship. Now part of his challenge is to attract the kind of talent that will keep Boeing innovative. As he moves into a new team, he boots up lessons gathered from exploring the RenGen.

Truly, technology has added millions of iterations to the bricks-and-mortar infrastructure to form an alternative system: a "long tail" (a term coined by Chris Anderson, author of *The Long Tail: Why the Future of Business Is Selling Less of More*). Our technological advances have expanded the universe of art and ideas. Some savvy marketers in the corporate world have

picked up the scent of shifting interests among the public and
have begun contributing their own venues and creative products
in the form of experiential marketing. To illustrate the point,
take the Illy Coffee Company, which set up an art gallery in New
York. They served coffee, yes, but the primary use of this expensive Manhattan square footage was to display art in such a way as
to borrow the power of the imagery for their brand by having it
coexist in the same environment. A company representative and
a bona fide art expert curated the show. You could drop in, look
around, hang out, and, oh, yes, have a cup of coffee.

This type of corporate contribution has fascinating implications for the world of art, something we'll explore later in the
book. For now, it is important to understand that there is abun-
dant demand for art and ideas manifested in everyday products
and settings.

Next, we'll take a more in-depth look at several companies
that are examples of RenGen principles at work. They range
from a gear manufacturer to an athletic apparel company, representing brands as pervasive as Starbucks and as noteworthy as
Absolut Vodka. Each offers a different strategy for applying the
lessons in this book to attain competitive advantage.

Early Adopter of the RenGen Aesthetic: How Absolut Vodka Conquered a Business Category

When Absolut Vodka began its landmark advertising campaign
nearly twenty years ago, the Swedish company simply wanted to
move more bottles of vodka. As it happened, Absolut revolutionized the drinking habits of millions.

By 2005, beer manufacturers woke up and discovered they had lost considerable market share to spirits, in particular vodka. *Advertising Age* magazine sent reporters into bars to find out why. Beer is considered "a bubba drink," they were told by the 30-something males who were sipping martinis in local watering holes. By June 2006, beer had lost its footing in its most sacred market—college campuses. In a survey of 100 U.S. universities by market research firm Student Monitor, beer drinking ranked well below iPod use and Facebook.com as the most popular things about college.

How Absolut managed to convert so many beer drinkers in America into vodka drinkers has little to do with people's palates. The magic was in the mind-set. Absolut built its brand based on a RenGen aesthetic, and in doing so conquered an industry and elevated its humble bottle into an icon.

By 1985, Absolut was five years into a campaign of print ads that featured its broad-shouldered bottle accompanied by simple slogans such as "ABSOLUT perfection." Stolichnaya, the leading vodka at the time, was feeling the heat. But the campaign, although stylish, was still conservative. Rather than wait for Stolichnaya to defend itself with its own volley of ads, the creative team at advertising agency TBWA that had invented the Absolut campaign had an inspiration. To magnify the brand's fashionable identity, they would link it with art. In his book about the campaign, Richard Lewis, one of the team members at the agency, describes what happened next.

The team met with Andy Warhol. Over dinner, Warhol said he was enthralled by the artfulness of the Absolut bottle. Warhol proposed painting his own interpretation of the bottle. He was paid $65,000 for the painting, "a price that would establish the ceiling for all future Absolut artists' works. In years to come, people in the agency would frequently say, about any one of a number of artists, 'He isn't worth more than Andy.'"

The idea was a bold one. After all, sales were humming along. Why not sit back and enjoy the ride? Indeed, some agency principals feared that the concept could bomb. The hand wringing led to a compromise: Warhol's depiction of the bottle would be placed in only a few publications with highly sophisticated readerships.

ABSOLUT WARHOL became a smash hit.

"Absolut Vodka had become a fashionable brand, and in Warhol's work, we saw an opportunity to accelerate the process," Lewis explains. The next goal was to use it as leverage to entice cultural consumers—Hollywood types, the rich, the famous, other artists—"who saw Warhol as something of a prophet, someone who would lead his friends to Absolut."

Until this time, no major advertiser had thought to use art as a primary marketing strategy. So delighted was Warhol by the response to his ad, he suggested doing a whole series of ABSO-LUT WARHOL paintings. But the agency had a better idea: It would ask Warhol to be their "seeing-eye dog" in the art world and to introduce them to new trends and rising art stars.

Just as Absolut commissioned artists to express the brand's cachet among trendsetters and opinion leaders, it enhanced the product's appeal by associating its bottle with fashion. The creative team found David Cameron, a young, talented, struggling fashion designer, who might be interested in doing something.

Cameron designed a simple silver minidress with the entire Absolut bottle copy on its front. Using a blond, athletically leggy model in action poses, the ads made the brand come alive. The response was directly expressed: Nearly 5,000 people called an 800 number that appeared in the ad's fine print. "Virtually all of the callers were women who wanted to purchase the dress. Reasoning that Absolut was in the fashion business as much as it was in the liquor business, we were momentarily tempted to reproduce Cameron's creation and sell it to the public, but wiser heads ultimately prevailed," Lewis writes.

In the decade that followed, Absolut would create associations with more fashion designers, as well as with film and literature. It had tapped into the isolation that bright, thoughtful people were feeling in a society that appeared to favor simplemindedness. With a trilogy of ads—ABSOLUT WELLS, ABSOLUT SHELLEY, and ABSOLUT STOKER—the brand honored the creators of *The Invisible Man*, *Frankenstein*, and *Dracula*. These were intended to be a niche set of ads for a very select group that ran in literary-minded publications such as the *New Yorker* and the *New York Times Book Review*. Understanding them takes a few seconds—maybe many seconds—even when the reader is on the appropriate wavelength and reading a magazine whose emphasis in on literature. Again, the risk paid off, as Lewis adds: "We hear time and again that people appreciate the challenge, particularly when they conquer it." This was a leap, not a step, and the brand opened the door to a larger audience than it had ever anticipated.

The Absolut story is a gold mine of trailblazing ideas. The unique ad campaign paved the way, not just for new drinking tastes but also for a new sensibility among people hungry to define themselves by an aesthetic of smart. If you believe, as I do, that we have become consumers of advertising messages as much as of the products they promote, then you can see how Absolut's brand has itself become iconic, predisposing people toward a new point of view.

Reebok International Aligns with RenGen Youth

Que Gaskins is vice president for youth and entertainment marketing at Reebok International Ltd. I met him at a marketing conference at Northwestern University's Kellogg School of Management, where he was a panelist discussing marketing strategy. The message he delivered immediately set him apart.

In answer to a question about how he was reaching the youth market, Gaskins offered up a snapshot of Reebok's progressive efforts to align with the "new culture of youth." He had walked the streets of Boston, interviewing young people about their interests, and had seen them come alive when they talked about their music, their poetry, their artwork. Here was a sporting goods company that realized it had to fuse sports imagery with art to remain relevant to the next generation of buyers. Reebok is embracing the RenGen and, in fact, helping speed it along.

After a period of "aerobics chic" in the 1980s, followed by "also-ran" status behind Nike, Reebok decided to take aim at the youth market. It hired Que Gaskins, and Reebok has been beyond cool ever since. An ardent believer in knowing the customer as a whole person, not just as a demographic statistic, he tracks youth trends by spending hours observing teens in public places like malls and community centers. He not only has predicted trends in youth culture but also helps drive them.

In a speech to a roomful of sponsorship marketing executives, Gaskins declared that "If the definition of insanity is doing exactly the same things but expecting different results, then, unfortunately, most marketers operate in a very insane manner in attempting to connect with consumers." He continued, "We expect to get new results from our advertising and other marketing campaigns, but for the most part, we employ the same tactics over and over. Marketers have tried to understand consumers by looking at them demographically: male, female, 12-to-17-year-olds, 18-to-30-year-olds, African American, Asian American and so on. But what we have found out is that consumers don't like to be put in neat little boxes, and that they don't actually fit in those boxes."

At Reebok, there is more interest in depth and breadth of customer insight. Gaskins explained, "Just because someone is an African American male who listens to rap music and loves basketball doesn't mean that an ad with rap music and basketball is going to hit the mark with him. Making a connection goes a lot deeper than that."

In the fall of 2005, Gaskins joined me on a panel to discuss the cultural consumer at a business breakfast sponsored by the *Boston Business Journal.* Following the event, he expressed interest in collaborating on the research I was doing that was the basis for this book. A spirited thinker and evangelist for following the road less traveled, Gaskins applied the concept of fusion from our research into Reebok's marketing approach. Gaskins likes to call it "fusionism."

What does *fusionism* mean?

It is the act of merging two or more elements involved in influencing consumers. It is forming a union between the ideas, styles, and tastes belonging to different cultures and different groups of people. Gaskins put it this way.

Fusionism happens any time a consumer steps out of one culture and incorporates part of another cultural lifestyle into his or her own, all the while maintaining a strong feeling of being an individual. Fusionism explains the rise in popularity of tattoos, acupuncture, and yoga, as well as the phenomenon of Eminem in rap and Lenny Kravitz in rock and roll. One of the great things about fusionism is that it addresses the dichotomy of people wanting to fit in while standing out. In today's culture, nobody wants to be plain, generic or boring; it's unacceptable. They want to celebrate what is different about themselves, but yet they still want to be part of something larger.

Gaskins understands that this perspective demands a liberated mind-set. It means understanding that people are being stimulated globally, and consequently are eliminating cultural boundaries and stereotypes. He thinks people in the marketing business are overdue for a fresh perspective on building relationships with consumers. Gaskins has the lifestyle profile of youth, for instance, down to a litany:

They like change and are always changing. They always want something new and different. They are spontaneous and want to experiment constantly. They celebrate their heritage but also are challenging of tradition. They are time-conscious. They are impatient. They are adventurous. They are smart. They are technology-oriented. They are curious. They seek authenticity. They are risk-oriented. They are elusive. They are image-conscious and they are realists.

This he knows. But his mantra, he told me, is "Never get too comfortable," which sends him constantly back to the streets to observe what's happening firsthand.

With the rise of technology, Gaskins observes that consumers pull influences from all over the world. "When young consumers can't find a certain shoe or album in a local store, they jump online and IM friends in Tokyo, Paris, and London to find out whether it is available there."

A few years ago, Reebok was in the perfect position to embrace the idea of fusionism, to apply a fresh perspective and do something unexpected in communicating with consumers. When I spoke with Gaskins about the next steps for Reebok as it builds a RenGen strategy, he was philosophical:

> The way forward is not to look ahead, but to look around. You can't get too comfortable. I ask kids where we should be. It is hard for adult marketers to really understand. Brands that break through are making decisions as dictated by teenagers. We have endorsement deals with people like 50 Cent. These people are not ideal as brand ambassadors because they are edgy, they are risk takers. But kids see things in these people that adults can't. Parents don't see this. Today, a straight-A student might be in a rock band. He might dress like he's not very successful. Parents want him to play classical music, so it makes them feel better as adults. But that is not the kid's standard of excellence.
>
> I have figured out that I must speak in cultural codes. Sometimes, it's more subtle, symbolic. Not all of it is in your face. It is not enough to have a Latino on your poster. You have to understand what the music means, what the language means, what the food means, what the sound means, so the customer ends up feeling, "Hey, they really understand me." So, the challenge becomes, how can we translate consumers' behaviors and create stories in our advertising and marketing that represent their attitude of exploration and discovery? We began by translating our positioning into a communicable theme: I Am What I Am.

Gaskins's campaign fused the physical strength appropriate to an athletic shoe with the soul of an artist and gave the ads a gritty edginess evocative of the indie outsider. It's one of

Reebok's most successful campaigns, and Gaskins believes he is tuned in to a cultural shift that has deeper roots. He has tapped the power of the RenGen.

Starbucks Brews Up Employee Loyalty with Art Production

The minute I walked into the Starbucks headquarters building in Seattle, I felt right at home. In every way, it was like an over-sized version of my local Starbucks store: warm cocoa colors on the walls, with red glass lamps hanging over plump sofas and chairs. As I waited in the lobby for the Starbucks spokesperson I was to meet, I took in the scene at the reception desk, where a friendly duo of male and female receptionists greeted people with the same earnest cheer of my local barista.

When she came to meet me, Anna Cunningham, program manager for corporate social responsibility programs, was no less cheerful. She led me up a flight of steel stairs and into a sprawling atrium with a gem-like slice of Puget Sound visible through the picture windows. We were there to discuss Starbucks's investment in social programs, and how these efforts have been advantageous to the company as well as the beneficiaries. I was especially interested in Starbucks's Make Your Mark program, which allows employees time off and, in some cases, grant monies to take on socially meaningful pursuits that benefit the community. Employees earn special points that can translate into cash or other rewards for the cause. Cunningham manages Make Your Mark as part of a broader portfolio of socially responsible initiatives.

A blond 30-something woman with soft features, Cunningham jumped in when I asked her the purpose of the program. "We are looking to grow and nurture young baristas. Whether they stay with Starbucks or not, if we encourage them to make things happen through their own initiative, we make the world a better place. We send that talent out there into the world. In the short term, the work of the community is also getting done. Long term, we make change in the world."

To tap into funding for Make Your Mark, Starbucks partners brew up an idea and present a plan. They are encouraged to be creative and develop an original idea; cookie-cutter franchise promotions are not what Starbucks is seeking here. Part of the benefit for the employees is the thrill of bringing something to life in their communities.

Make Your Mark took an artful turn in 2005 when a group of Starbucks partners in Chicago invented Avante Grande, a Starbucks-sponsored gallery show for employees who moonlight as visual artists. Just as with a regular art exhibition, the artworks were selected by a jury. Starbucks gave it street cred by booking it into a gallery on the gritty fringes of the more-established gallery district. The show was advertised in local newspapers, and on posters and postcards in stores. Serious art critics were invited. "It was an amazingly successful project," Cunningham said. "New York and Portland ended up replicating the concept, which very seldom happens, so it tells you how powerful the idea is."

The success of Avante Grande reflects not only on the ingenuity of Starbucks as a company—letting employee creativity take flight—but it also points to a RenGen reality. With more young artists pouring into the economy, and precious few opportunities for them to make a living doing their art, compromises will need to be made. Because of what we know about the creative personality, these artists are typically well-educated, inner-driven, and willing to work hard for the right incentives. That's what makes them attractive to employers. Essentially, Starbucks created the platform for employee innovation and self-expression through Avante Grande. It is the kind of initiative that makes a RenGen employee tick, and the broad concept is likely to gain ground in other industries.

But will it keep employees around?

I asked Cunningham if she thought the program might make people more loyal to their barista careers. She thought for a moment. "It's hard to say what exactly keeps people loyal. We had a few partners (employees) celebrate their twentieth anniversaries recently. Our benefits are generous, our philosophy is progressive. Our people feel a part of something that is a part of them."

For Starbucks, this is proving to be a rich blend.

Winzeler Gear Company Leaps from
Laggard to Leader by Getting Creative

From the outside, there is nothing remarkable about the Winzeler Gear Co. It is located in a light-industrial complex near the Kennedy Expressway, in the meat-and-potatoes suburb of Harwood Heights near Chicago. The company's plant is a low-slung building that covers the entire block. And when I entered, I could see through a series of glass doors into an atrium. I did a double-take: Just off the manufacturing floor was a large art gallery, and on display there was a dress made of plastic gears, by artist Cat Chow, the artist who fabricates sculptural garments by using everyday, yet unconventional, materials such as zippers, dollar bills, wire, O-rings—and Winzeler gears.

John Winzeler, the company's president and CEO, greeted me with a solid handshake and a courtly manner. In his early sixties, he sported a laid-back-yet-expensive look that I would expect to find in an advertising agency rather than a factory. Winzeler is an engineer by training, an art lover in his spare time, and a pragmatist when it comes to moving the family gear-making business forward. Still, he has found that by treating the work like an art form, he has earned a reputation, especially among European buyers, that has kept his gears spinning off the production line, while his U.S. competitors have lost out to cheaper offshore operations.

Winzeler Gear—the successor to a business founded nearly a century ago by Winzeler's grandfather—produces precision-molded plastic gears used in a myriad of products. For example, when you sit in your car and push the button to move the seat back, it's likely that one of Winzeler's gears helps make that happen.

John Winzeler's business philosophy is simple: The key to happiness is combining your work and your passion. "I've spent a lot of time trying to understand how I got to where I am today," said Winzeler, who once raced boats. Always mechanically minded, he described his earlier ambitions without any sense of regret. "When I was a young boy, I dreamed about working on cars and boats because my father did that. I was always dreaming about what I wanted the cars and boats to look like. I was always conceptualizing colors and shapes. I probably should have been a product designer instead of an engineer. But the family business was something tangible that I could help shape, to bring to its next stage of life. That mattered to me."

Winzeler decided to join the family business and looked for ways to integrate his interest in color and concept; his eye for design is evident throughout the manufacturing plant, whose construction he oversaw. "The theme of our building is gears. We try to use gears in an artful way so it's something we can enjoy, while leaving no doubt about what we do." Winzeler pointed to a row of windows covered with transparencies featuring representations of gears made from everything from a mosaic to a tattoo to an X-ray. He explained that he didn't want neighbors to peer into the eighteen windows while construction was underway during the plant expansion. So he commissioned an artist to cover the windows. Work by other artists can be found throughout the plant.

Winzeler's company approaches the process of making gears as a collaboration. Each project is undertaken in partnership with both customers and suppliers. After discussing the customer's vision and the design challenges involved, employees draw upon creative thinking and technical expertise, often tapping the resources of the company's strategic partners, to design products to suit the project at hand.

This approach to designing gears meshes well with Winzeler's aesthetic sensibilities. While he has always had an eye for fashion (he's been selecting his wife Carol's wardrobe for thirty-six years) and color, his formal introduction to the world of art began with a blank wall about ten years ago. With their children away at college, he and his wife had to make a decision: Remodel their home or move? They fell in love with a rambling 1950s ranch house. "We bought this home and started all over again in terms of furnishing it," he related. "We started with a mattress on the floor and a picnic table in the kitchen. We had these large white walls with nothing on them. At the time, [Chicago's] Museum of Contemporary Art was doing a fundraising campaign for a new building. We made commitments to the building fund, and that opened opportunities to meet living artists and view private collections." The Winzelers were exposed to art, architecture, and other creative media. "We began to travel somewhat to major shows, which has given us a whole new perspective. That brought out a need for being around art and other aesthetically beautiful things like furniture and music."

This journey led to a collaboration between the gear maker and artist Cat Chow that resulted in the gear dress I'd seen in the gallery just off the company's otherwise-modest reception area. Having once worked as a chain-mail fabricator for Renaissance fairs, Chow uses a related linking process for industrial or found materials. Chow uses the convention of the garment as a medium to make subtle allusions to traditional fashion modes, such as "the white wedding dress" made entirely of zippers.

The relationship between art, fashion, and industrial parts reflects the kind of fusion of materials and concepts so common to the RenGen. Although examples of crossover in modern art are found in the Surrealist experiments of Salvador Dali and, from the fashion world in Issey Miyake's sculptural fashions, Chow's primary intention for her garments is not that they be worn, but staged as sculpture. By transforming mundane materials like Kleenex into the stuff of formal elegance, Chow prompts us to question easy notions of what is beautiful. The shock of recognizing these common materials in the service of elegant sculptural forms, and the wit of their combinations, further challenge our assumptions about beauty in the common objects surrounding us.

Having indulged his fascination with art by working directly with artists, Winzeler now can't get enough. "For me to survive today, I need to be around a lot of creative people. I look for situations to be around a creative process, and that creative process might be designing a part. I enjoy being around art and getting to know local artists. This is a nice way to go forward. I've blossomed."

Just as visitors to the Winzeler plant get a first impression from the gear dress, employees get a similar first impression when they come to work each morning. Lining a wall of the employee entrance is a series of photos of fashion models wearing jewelry made from plastic gears. The photos originally were the focal point of a series of advertisements that ran in gear-industry magazines, and that earned the company a second look from prospects. Winzeler said the photos were hung at the employee entrance "so [workers] would feel the same positive impression of their workplace that customers feel when they walk in the front door."

"From the moment you come in the front door," he added, "we do not look like a manufacturing plant. We want it that way. We are hoping to attract the right kind of employee, someone who is creative and energized by the unexpected."

Winzeler hopes that by linking art and manufacturing, his workplace will be infused with an aesthetic appreciation. "I hope I've sensitized [our employees] to quality and beauty. I want them to see that it's important that something not only works, but looks good."

Winzeler also promotes his unorthodox approach to manufacturing through a scholarship he funds at his alma mater, Bradley University in Peoria, Illinois, and through frequent collaborations with students and faculty from the School of the Art Institute of Chicago.

But, ever the steady businessman, Winzeler said, "We're still in the manufacturing business; I have no illusions about that. We make and sell gears, and we have to do that well or none of this would matter. But people who visit tell us they find our environment stimulating, and they see the creativity of our engineers and technicians who create new processes . . . that sets us apart."

The concept is a layering on, not an overturning of the status quo. It must have elements that are foundational for it to succeed—technical ability, core skills, special insights and processes. Thomas Friedman's book *The World Is Flat* points to a balance between creativity and basic skills of literacy and numeracy. Friedman quotes Bill Gates as saying, "I have never met the guy who doesn't know how to multiply who created software." Ren-Genners will not forsake basic skills for some "creative" fantasyland where no one does homework and never has to learn long division. Rather, today's RenGen organizations draw upon existing strengths and an eruption of new ideas drawn from the high-stakes engagement with a world on the brink of a renaissance.

CHAPTER ELEVEN

The Catalytic People of a Renaissance

In our culture, the belief that one can be or accomplish anything, provided they try hard enough, is pervasive. However, as I stood in front of Michelangelo's *David* during my research trip to Florence, I was struck by a different truth: talent is not democratic. Some people are born with extraordinary abilities. Do they study and develop their craft? Unequivocally yes. Do they work hard? Certainly. They study, practice, and develop their skills just like the rest of us. But unlike most of us, they achieve astonishing feats.

Talent has many facets. Sometimes talent lies in the intangible qualities of charisma, vision, or bravery. In a renaissance, particular people with a certain combination of talents rise to prominence in the society. This chapter is about the personality types commonly found to facilitate a renaissance. It is not clear whether the pressure of the decline that precedes a renaissance hones these talents or just inspires them to emerge. Nor is there always a linear path of ascendancy. The main thing to know is that without the right mixture of these talents, it is unlikely that a renaissance can blossom. These people are human catalysts. Some of them boldly cut new paths, while others are like enzymes that act as catalysts. Either way, they constitute the human alchemy of the RenGen.

The Master Patron

There is no renaissance without art. There is no art without patrons. Unhindered by social conventions, the master patron in any period of history is politically connected at the highest levels, socially prominent, and has access to colossal amounts of wealth. One individual that embodies the RenGen model of master patron is John Bryan, chairman of the Sara Lee Corporation. In 2000, Chicago mayor Richard M. Daley and John Bryan sat down to look at the drawings for Chicago's Millennium Park project. The plan was to turn a gritty rail-yard eyesore into a jewel of a public park. The vision was an ambitious undertaking that would change the face of downtown Chicago and redefine the urban park as a place where everyday people could experience high art for free.

I first encountered John Bryan in the late 1980s when I worked at the Art Institute of Chicago, where he was a trustee. At an event for businesspeople, Mr. Bryan recalled his first business trip in England, where he'd accompanied Nathan Cummings, founder and then CEO of Sara Lee Corporation. Having finished their business for the day, Mr. Cummings asked the driver to take them to the home and studio of sculptor Henry Moore. Then a young executive, Mr. Bryan knew a little about the art world. By contrast, Nathan Cummings was a connoisseur, the kind of collector other collectors follow.

It was in Henry Moore's studio that John Bryan fell in love with art. As he told the story that afternoon, his voice caught ever so slightly. People in the audience leaned closer, unsure if they had heard it or not. After all, here was a titan of industry, publicly revealing an emotion for which he was utterly unashamed.

I spoke with John Bryan about his role in Chicago's Millennium Park project. First of all, I wanted to know how the vision for the park came to be. "I was asked to raise the funds," he recalls. "The mayor had plans drawn up to revitalize the park, and had to figure out how to pay for the architect's drawings."

But when the mayor called John Bryan, he got more than a commitment to champion the park project. "I looked at those drawings and told the mayor that I had to see some magic in the idea or we'd have trouble raising serious money."

After some thought, Bryan "took the charge and helped define the park." He decided to use the very highest-level talent to create the most extraordinary environment in the park and in doing so to "make a statement about Chicago to the world," says Bryan. "There are ten cities who claim they have they have the best symphony, opera, and art museum." Bryan understood he had to step up and stand out from that pack to achieve the status he was aiming for with his plan. He got to work. First he mobilized an art committee to help choose the sculpture. Next came a garden committee, and so on. "We went to the people in town with serious money, and we let them be a part of the grand plan."

Believing there was something valuable in having a big name attached to the project, John Bryan approached architect Frank Gehry to design the band shell. Gehry turned him down flat. Undaunted, Bryan approached a member of the wealthy Pritzker family. If he had the project paid for in advance, he thought he could woo Gehry, who had come off of a string of projects that had gone well over budget and left their financiers between a brick and a metal plate. Bryan secured the money from Cindy Pritzker, who agreed to fund the project, and Gehry accepted.

As the project took shape, Bryan ended up in the most desirable situation imaginable. People came to him with money. "I ended up getting calls from people who wanted to contribute $1 million. That was about 100 people."

What mix of talents and conditions are required to make a project on such a grand scale succeed? "It's a confluence of quite a lot of things," Bryan says. "Location—the spot between the Lake and Michigan Avenue, right next to the Art Institute is really unbeatable. Enlightened government—having a mayor with vision helps a great deal. A prosperous population and a strong economy help. Chicago is more prosperous than many cities. Many people have made their fortunes in this city and have pride in that. Finally, I guess, it helps to be solving a problem—in our case it was getting rid of an eyesore."

When I ask if the project lived up to the original vision, I can hear the smile in Bryan's voice. "Everyone tells me they love it. And the downtown has seen the doggonedest renaissance you ever saw." Indeed the park is attracting tourists from all over the world, along with new restaurants and condo buildings, as the strip of Michigan Avenue that was once a dead zone but is now the toniest address in the city.

But has it improved the quality of life for those in the city?

"We brought the world's greatest art and architecture to a public park. Providing upscale offerings to everyone for free was very important to all of us. We sought to appeal to the higher instincts of people. It seems to be working. You have to offer it first, and people, as it turns out, end up enjoying it. It lifts them up."

As for the future, I ask him about the arts community's concern about there being no replacements for the John Bryans and the David Rockefellers among the younger set of business leaders. Will there be any more corporate philanthropists of his kind? Bryan concedes that the tradition of corporate patronage is subsiding. "I preach the gospel that it is worthy and worthwhile for companies to share their largess. . . . Companies have been less generous."

But there is something else taking its place, he tells me, and that is entrepreneurial wealth. Bryan brightens, and says, "It is hard to distinguish between corporate and private money. Many of today's entrepreneurs are using their personal wealth." Rather than a vestige of an old tradition, it is possible to see Bryan as a guiding light in the rebirth of civic values in the private sector—a rebirth that echoes RenGen values.

Personalities like Bryan are rare in any civilization. They combine an unbounded vision with a power base that makes them immune to petty compromises and naysayers. Without master patrons, grand plans collect dust on paper, and a city's reach never exceeds its grasp. Simply, no renaissance ever occurs without master patrons like John Bryan; they are the leavening ingredient that makes everything rise.

The Expressives

The flowering of a RenGen is accompanied by a flurry of creative productivity from complete amateurs. People who get swept into the artistic current and begin writing poetry, painting, reading and sharing ideas for the fun of it, even costuming themselves to play a role as a creative person, are behaviors that crop up in abundance. In ordinary times these populations wax and wane, and their behavior is what we call trendy.

Some expressives aspire to make their living as artists and are drawn into art schools and have brief art careers. For others, their interests get put on hold and they may loop back and around depending on what else is occurring in their lives: schooling, jobs, family. But they never lose their affinity for creative expression and, important, they become the consumer base for creative product.

This is the segment of the population that is driving participation in face pages, blogs, and low-budget video competitions. Customer-made advertisements are another nice example of expressives in action. Trendwatching, a global consumer trend advisory, explains it this way: "The phenomenon of corporations creating goods, services, and experiences in close cooperation with experienced and creative consumers, tapping into their intellectual capital, and in exchange giving them a direct say in what actually gets produced, manufactured, developed, designed, serviced, or processed." This phenomenon relies on the segment of people who delight in expressing their creativity; and it turns out the pool is large and growing.

This ever-expanding pool of expressives, facilitated by the Internet and other low- and no-skill means of image production, is creating a new genre of marketing that actively puts the customer in the driver's seat. In some cases, literally. Volkswagen's Gypsy Cab Project selected, out of a pack of applicants, a young filmmaker from Denver to drive a cab and film the action. He drives a specially marked VW Rabbit around New York City picking up free fares and recording the interactions on tape. The goal is to hit 100 fares in fourteen days, and, as of this writing, eleven episodes have been posted at Gypsycabproject.com. The videos of the fares were posted as the saga unfolded. Test drives, drama, Web-tv, and product placement all rolled into one helped VW restage the Rabbit. Since the expressives represent a large segment of the RenGen, it is likely that they will produce more self-created content, incorporating their creative interests into all types of other lifestyle behaviors including shopping, dating, dining, and socializing.

The Auteur

The French word for *author* is *auteur*. It describes an artist of some success, one who has not achieved perhaps the enduring notoriety of a Master Artist, nor the proliferation, but an auteur shows the way to another level of artistry. The personality of the auteur builds a following and remains somewhat accessible to aspirants, easily incorporating younger people into their sphere of influence. They achieve their status by leaving a personal stamp on their work that makes it uniquely their own. Filmmaker Tim Burton, the late artist Keith Haring, and performance artist Laurie Anderson are examples of auteurs.

The Young Auteurs

I opened the *Wall Street Journal* one day to find a story about Keegan McHargue who makes acrylic-on-paper paintings that sell as fast as he can paint them. There was also mention of a Rosson Crow who has a waiting list for her paintings, which sell for as much as $16,000. Or Ryan Trecartin, whose video art pieces have been screened in major museums. "But for all these accolades, there's one thing these artists haven't achieved yet: a twenty-sixth birthday," notes reporter Kelly Crow.

What's happening here? The economic good times of the knowledge economy has met the warm front of a RenGen aesthetic and made rain for many young artists. The revved-up market forces that favor authentic, original work are heating up supply and demand. Collectors are keenly hedging their bets that one of these artists will turn out to be the next Andy Warhol and worth millions. So, rather than waiting and working a lifetime to be discovered, these aspiring expressives have now become auteurs, almost overnight.

This quickened pace has had a ripple affect. In 2006, at the Whitney Museum of American Art's influential biennial showcase for contemporary art, twelve of the 101 featured artists were in their twenties—double the number from its previous show. Art school grads with as much (or perhaps more) business savvy than artistic talent, are becoming their own art dealers by promoting their work through classmates and friends.

Art school MFA thesis shows are being attended by ever larger hordes of buyers, as well as the media. In fact, some art schools have had to determine strict protocols for the purchasing student artwork. When the Yale's MFA program originally launched a daylong open house where outsiders could roam the studios filled with student works, the attendance was rarely higher than 100. Now, three times that many are showing up, says Peter Halley the director of Yale's painting department. To accommodate the interest, the next event will be stretched out over two days. In another example, tickets for the School of the Art Institute of Chicago's Annual Fashion Show of student designs sell out in a matter of days, and a private shopping event follows the show.

As the RenGen gears up, there's keen interest in spotting emerging talent balanced by an interest in credentialing it; thus, giving the art a cachet that warrants the investment. Hence, the term *auteur* is on the rise.

Let's switch tracks to the music scene, where young artists are also being granted *auteur* status. In 2006, the *New York Times Sunday Magazine* devoted a spread to Danger Mouse—aka Brian Burton, who is also one half of the music duo Gnarls Barkley. At the time the article appeared, Danger Mouse/Gnarls Barkley. had a hit album *St. Elsewhere*, and a chart-topping single, "Crazy," with an accompanying video that morphed Rorschach-like images to Danger Mouse beats. It was a cerebral display of RenGen artistry.

Danger Mouse personifies the RenGen fusion aesthetic. He is a multidisciplinary artist with a knack for fusing pop, hip-hop, soul, and rock in collaborations with fellow artists that employ referential hooks to, as Klosterman puts it. Burton makes "people realize musical connections they never knew existed." This union of two cultures is something he comes by naturally. Growing up in a predominantly Jewish neighborhood in Spring Valley, New York, his family was one of only two black ones. "My parents didn't tell me anything about why I was different," he insists. "I think that was good. I had no idea why I looked the way I looked, so I had to use my imagination."

Because this renaissance happens in the warp speed that is the twenty-first century, it is no surprise that acclaim occurs earlier for artists—moving them swiftly from aspiring expressive to auteurs. And the news is largely good—it allows them to pay off student loans and rent or, in some cases, mortgage studio space so they themselves are economic drivers.

Portrait of a Budding Auteur

Gwynn Cassidy has moved through the expressive stage and, depending on her vision and contribution, may prove to be an auteur. I was introduced to Gwynn by one of my cultural scouts, Marj Halperin. Gwynn is a 36-year-old writer and producer of various media with an emphasis on Web-based projects and a concentration on women's issues. She studied filmmaking at New York University and worked as a documentary filmmaker before joining iVillage as a beauty editor.

In March 2005, Cassidy founded Women Work the Web, a network of women's online businesses. Her first project, the REAL Hot 100, is what Cassidy calls a "media justice project" designed to promote positive images of younger women in the popular media. It is a takeoff on *Maxim*'s Hot 100 that selects women for their physical attributes, but instead, it rewards women for their brains and social contributions rather than their cleavage. Her second project, Girls in Government, was set to launch when she spoke to me from her New York apartment. The new organization works to mobilize younger women around issues of government, democracy, and justice. Her day job is as a Webmaster at the national Association of Women's Legal Momentum Fund. In her spare time, Gwynn serves on the board of the New York Younger Women's Task Force as the director of communications of the New York Metro Region and volunteers as a Big Sister, an S.A.T. tutor, and develops Web sites for select nonprofits.

"I made a conscious choice to set up my life so that I could work for a responsible organization to pay the rent, volunteer, and build projects that help me contribute in some way to the things I care about changing." Sounds ideal, but Cassidy gave up a lot. She expresses no regret. "I left the corporate world to have this life. I trust myself to make the right choices for me. When I had a real job, I watched my pregnant colleagues panic when their maternity leaves were cut in half. I thought no way am I going to let that happen to me. So I took control and built a life that, if someday, I decide to be a mom, I have some flexibility."

Gwynn's life is a RenGen collage of community service, writing, producing, project management, organizing, and networking. She is self-directed, driven, and very interested in contributing her talent in a way that improves the world. And she refuses to give up the many facets of her identity that fuse to make her whole: by her own definition, she is a girlie girl, feminist, leader, mentor, and perhaps someday, she hopes, a mother.

The Master Planner

The renaissance context does not just bubble up—it has planners. These are individuals with a rare combination of skills; they are emotionally intelligent, visionary, and practical. They usually have training in art, engineering, or architecture and work collaboratively behind the scenes to establish the urban environments that give context to a renaissance.

Here's an example from history. Donato Bramante was the mastermind behind Rome's ambitious reconstruction in the late Renaissance. Bramante began his career as a painter and in 1499, he moved to Rome, where he came to the attention of the future Pope Julius II who engaged Bramante to lead the renewal of the Vatican complex. In his buildings, Bramante experimented with illusionist features that altered the sense of perspective. But his importance historically is the way he advanced large-scale projects, one after another, to shape a city. Bramante's legacy is felt less in the buildings he personally designed and constructed than in the way he influenced people. He inspired young artists, managed master artists and their difficult temperaments, fundraised from politicians and popes, and schooled successive architects.

Bramante was a city planner before such a job existed, and he was someone whose talent had a long arc across history, inspiring many who would follow. RenGen urban planners John Rahaim of Seattle and Ty Tabing of Chicago, who will be profiled in the next chapter on second cities, share many of Bramante's traits of soaring vision, winning personalities, and pragmatic tenacity for slogging through the mess of making a city flourish.

The Instigator

As the word suggests, *instigators* are the people who catalyze things. Unlike master patrons and auteurs, they may or may not have creative talents or means of their own, and they may or may not be good fundraisers. They may or may not have authoritative positions in the artistic community, such as a board membership. But regardless of means or position, instigators all have one thing in common: they possess an attracting principle that draws in and inspires artists, supporters, and other individuals. Instigators are masterful conveners capable of filling the room with just the right people and orchestrating introductions so that next-step conversations can occur.

I sat down with Peter Donnelly at a coffee shop in an area of Seattle that is undergoing a development boom. Occasionally, construction sounds gave off a shuddering thud. The sun was out—a noteworthy detail in Seattle—and a shaft of sunlight fell across Donnelly's face; I could see how his thick gray hair and puckish smile give him a boyish look despite his age.

Peter Donnelly is one part impresario and two parts power broker. He came to Seattle at the time of the World's Fair and watched the upstart city raise the bar with the construction of landmarks like the Space Needle. He also had a hand in the building boom of new cultural venues that coincided with the Fair.

When he first arrived in Seattle, Donnelly's first job was as the head of a regional theatre company. It was an ambitious time in American theatre. An exodus had begun out of New York, shooting five-star talent into cities like Minneapolis, Seattle, San Francisco, and Chicago. "We were a generation looking for a new artistic model, and that meant a new business model," says Donnelly. He described the New York theatre scene of that period as a closed system run by investors and Broadway moguls. "This began a great decentralization of performing arts. It meant that cities like Seattle could develop and produce indigenous work using local casts. Audiences were emancipated from the routine road shows of Broadway productions with second-string casts. Americans were thereby exposed to high-quality productions of important plays." What Donnelly describes is akin to a new distribution system for a more challenging repertoire of live theatre made available to more audiences.

At the pinnacle of Donnelly's career, he led a united arts fund that operates much like a United Way for the Seattle arts community. Today, Donnelly sees Seattle as a city poised for its next wave of ambition. "We have the infrastructure of wealth, thanks to companies like Microsoft, Amazon, and Starbucks. And we have the ambition," he says.

However, I was determined to know more about what specifically he thinks lies ahead for Seattle, given that it is still very much an upstart city.

Donnelly asserts that Seattle will experience another major boom. "We have the intellectual and creative temperament. People love to talk and think here. Our bookstores are crowded. People actually stay after theatre performances for discussions with the actors. People are ambitious and we can build what we dream. We have proven it." Donnelly points out the window at the Space Needle. "I can't imagine a more elegant symbol of modern confidence," he says.

Instigators like Peter Donnelly have one thing in common: they make things happen by creating excitement. Over time, they build a power base and they learn shortcuts to getting things done, even if it means bending the rules a bit. In all cases they are charismatic, attracting supporters and managing contention with diplomacy so that whenever possible, they leave no enemies in their wake. Why? Because unlike master patrons, they have limited power and they themselves do not possess great wealth. Their primary resource is their own passion and they wield it to draw other people into the action.

The Master Artist

Master artists are major players in a RenGen. They stand at the pinnacle of talent and achievement. They are recognized in their times, and their work is sought after. Most important, such artists rise through the ranks from expressive to aspirant to auteur. If there is not a large enough pool of talent in these preceding ranks, there will be very few masters or none at all. Master talent is most prominent near the apex of a renaissance. The rarest of these masters have talents that cross over several disciplines, such as art and science, architecture and sculpture, and music and mathematics; Leonardo da Vinci is a prime example.

How does this type of person play a role in today's RenGen? Consider for a moment the master artist Mikhail Baryshnikov, the Russian American dancer. While he still performs and teaches, at 57, he is at the age when most dancers retire from the boards altogether. Instead, he founded the Baryshnikov Arts Center in Manhattan, where he says that he "hopes to make life better for performing artists." The center inaugurated fellowships for young artists, who are given studio space, technological support (light, sound, video), and some money to get their shows together. They are also assigned mentors of their choosing. For example, the playwright Edwin Sanchez worked with Anton Dudley, a recent graduate of the theatre program at NYU's Tisch School. The center encourages cross-disciplinary collaborations like the one between Tere O'Connor, the veteran downtown choreographer, and Jamie Allen, a multimedia artist who put together a complicated dance-cum-video production. Also in operation is a program that offers residencies to mid-career artists, allowing them to work, at no cost, in big, clean, airy studios. In all

disciplines—dance, music, modern architecture, computer animation, filmmaking, sculpture, or literary art—there are master
artists with talent to lead a renaissance.

The Connoisseur

As you might imagine, a connoisseur is the ultimate trained pal-
ette, the tastemaker who is emulated by other collectors. They
tend to be mature and have great wealth. They acquire art and
hold a place on the way to becoming a master patron, who is in
all cases also a connoisseur.

Profile of a Connoisseur:
Agostino Chigi—The Pope's Banker

I walked amid the buzzing Vespas of Travestere, a neighborhood in Rome across from the Tiber River, to find the urban
mansion that once belonged to Agostino Chigi, banker to the
papacy during the high-Italian Renaissance. The immensely
wealthy Chigi was a patron of the arts during the reigns of both
Pope Julius II and Pope Leo X, the period when Michelangelo
created the Sistine Chapel frescoes and Raphael painted the inner
apartments of the Vatican. In fact, Chigi loaned large sums to the
papacy to complete the Sistine Chapel, and he had a hand in
launching Raphael as an artist in Rome, paying him handsomely
to paint a fresco of Chigi's zodiac chart in his mansion. (The
belief that the constellation of the stars at the hour of a man's
birth dictates a man's destiny was common in the Renaissance.)

In the era of Pope Julius II, Chigi controlled the vast enter-
prises of the papacy, including the lucrative alum mines that

supplied the fixative for wool dyes. It was the pope's cash cow. Chigi also raised armies, traveled in secrecy bearing the demands of an ambitious pope to foreign kings, and helped negotiate sensitive alliances with the baronial families who ruled the powerful citystates of Venice and Florence.

Chigi matured into a master patron in the time of Pope Leo X, encouraging all forms of art and expression. Chigi financed a printing press for Rome. He gave poets of the day clerkships in his bank and commissioned all types of written work, from speeches to poems, as part of the lavish celebrations held in his home. As Felix Gilbert writes in *The Pope, His Banker, and Venice*: "The banquets Chigi gave for the Pope and visiting princes were famous for the magnificence; ambassadors reported about them to their governments with admiration tinted only by a little disgust." It was told that after each course of the meal the silver was thrown into the Tiber. It was also said that Chigi ordered nets placed below the surface of the water so that fisherman could gather the silver and return it the next morning.

Unhindered by social conventions, Agostino Chigi was a connoisseur who provided the means by which Italian art of the period could flourish. Equivalent players in the RenGen come in all shapes and sizes, and while they are all extremely rich, not all are billionaires. Their tastes vary as well from iconic art to landscapes. Most of their collections are sequestered in privacy, like those of publisher S.I. Newhouse, hedge-fund king Steven A. Cohen, or software giant Bill Gates. Barnes & Noble founder and chairman Leonard Riggio, although not a billionaire, favors minimalist art and also chairs one of the great enablers of contemporary art, the DIA Foundation. Some connoisseurs open their collections to the public, such as home-building and insurance tycoon Eli Broad's Broad Art Foundation in Santa Monica, California.

Forbes magazine reports in its 2006 roundup of the "Modern Medicis" that "We have been living through an astounding boom—one that far surpasses its predecessor of the later 1980s."

Since the business of collecting art is often transacted behind the scenes, it is hard to know who else might be out there quietly investing. For now, it is important to know that the cadre of connoisseurs is active and wealthy enough to keep buying for some time, a fact that also sets the stage for the RenGen.

The human context of a renaissance is important. When the seven personalities—the Expressives, the Auteurs, the Connoisseurs, the Instigators, the Master Artists, the Master Patrons, and the Master Planners—converge in the right setting, with enough interplay to flavor and inspire each other, and when external conditions prevail to raise the stakes—the conditions are ripe for a renaissance.

CHAPTER TWELVE

Second Cities of the Renaissance

When asked about cultural meccas in the United States, many Americans tend to think of cities like New York or Los Angeles and their venerable cultural institutions such as the Lincoln Center and the Getty Museum. However, a renaissance starts in *second cities*. Just as Florence and to a lesser extent, Milan, were hothouses for the Italian renaissance, instead of Rome, the RenGen is more visible in cities such as Chicago, Seattle, Providence, and Philadelphia (though these cities are by no means an exclusive list of where the RenGen is occurring).

This chapter is about the places where the RenGen is gearing up. Major cities like Los Angeles or New York, despite their cultural infrastructure or creative output, are too established to really be considered part of the upstart movement of the RenGen. And then, there was the matter of conflicting information. Our research team was confused when, for instance, Richard Florida's favorite "creative class" cities ranked poorly in other economic measures, such as how well they hatch high-growth companies. Thus, we examined cities that fascinated us in a variety of ways. Though doing this required us to relax our methodology just a bit, the cities profiled in this chapter were examined using the following criteria:

1. **People.** The city has to have "catalytic people" actively engaged in helping to make things happen.

2. **Ways to learn.** The city must include intellectual infrastructure such as museums, educational institutions, libraries, apprenticeship programs, and the like to allow people at various stages in life to adapt intellectually.

3. **Density.** The urban core has to be dense, increasing the likelihood that people will interact, thereby improving the likelihood that ideas could be exchanged and connections made.

4. **Circulatory system.** Density without movement is a recipe for stagnation. Pedestrian walkways, river boats, public transportation, bicycle paths, and well-planned thoroughfares all keep the blood flow of a city pumping.

5. **Green initiatives.** Environmentally progressive cities have a leg up from the start. They inspire a sense of confidence that enormous issues can be addressed by human beings.

6. **Affordability.** The city has to be livable for that class of creative people, no matter what their discipline or purpose.

7. **Civitas.** Romans used the term to encompass a general sense of orderly living where native tribes were friendly and local government carried out civil administration of public land, buildings, and streets.

The affordability factor garnered particular attention in our research. More than anything else, this factor ruled out New York and Los Angeles. While there is always some sense of financial struggle for the freelance-based creatives—according to U.S. Bureau of Labor statistics, 1 in 100 people make a living from an art form—in expensive cities like New York, the cost of living has meant a near diaspora for the creative sector. The Freelancer's Union of New York reported that in 2006, "over 40 percent of its members reported making less than $35,000 last year, half have little to no personal savings, and over a third lack proper health insurance." High-priced rents alone can kill creativity; ambitious ideas have to be scaled back to be contained in tiny apartments instead of airy lofts. Context matters in a renaissance, but adaptability does, too, so New York's loss proved to be Philadelphia's gain—as you will discover from our profiles of RenGen cities.

Seattle

Seattle is a wired city. It's home to one of the biggest technology companies on the planet (Microsoft), and it has a thirst for caffeinated drinks that doesn't let up. It's also a youthful city. The median age in Seattle is under 36, which gives it an optimistic vibe. It's a city that has started to put down some historic roots as an iconic American place. Moreover, Seattle is growing like crazy. The city plans for forty-nine new large buildings to be completed over the next four years—some commercial, but many residential and located in the core of Seattle's Center City.

To understand more of what's behind this massive building boom, I sat down with John Rahaim, the Planning Director for the City of Seattle since August 2003. Modest about his biography, he waved away my enthusiasm for his previous accomplishments—founding CityDesign, the city's office of Urban Design, or for his role as an editor of *Arcade* magazine. Instead, he showered his staff and coworkers with praise. "It takes a whole team of people to make civic things happen," he told me.

The Emerald City lives green

Over dinner in a snug bistro adjacent to the Pike Place Market, I explain the RenGen research project, and John Rahaim lights immediately on one of Seattle's defining characteristics: the environmental ethic of the region. As he says, "It's evolved into a movement about how we can sustainably live together on the planet." The conversations are no longer about recycling or smoking bans. They focus on growth management for the city and how to control urban sprawl.

Rahaim quickly explains that Seattle is the first city in the nation to be certified by the U.S. Green Building Council. He notes, "We have more green buildings than any other city in the country." And his department has even set up a Green Building Team to ensure that future public, commercial, or residential homes understand the environmental, social, and economic benefits to building green. "It's the triple bottom line," Rahaim notes, "but city leaders started it right as development was taking off, back in 1998." They didn't wait for federal guidelines or ask for permission—they just started doing it.

Center City Seattle

The project that dominates Rahaim's time now is the Center City Project. It's the mayor's strategy for Seattle's downtown core and the nine neighborhoods around it to be livable and walkable 24/7. It's all about protecting and enhancing the quality inside the city boundary—rather than outside, as is custom in most cities. As expected, the project features green spaces where the pedestrian is king. The project includes "upzoning," which removes the height restriction for buildings downtown. It also reconnects the central waterfront by removing the Alaskan Way viaduct. John Rahaim explains that these improvements will create a high-quality, high-density environment where people can live, work, and raise a family downtown.

Good thing—because it is projected that by 2024, there will be 100,000 new residents and 84,000 new jobs in Seattle.

Open access, free for all: Seattle Public Library

The gleaming new Seattle Public Library is the city's latest icon. It captures a blend of RenGen aesthetics with its wraparound views of Seattle's natural beauty and provocative public art. Rem Koolhaas's 11-floor, 362,987-square-foot design has won awards and the city's heart for a beautiful new place to read, learn, and find information. The controversial design was declared by the *Seattle Times* as "arguably the most striking and imaginative piece of Seattle architecture since the Space Needle."

The Seattle Public Library's mission, as described on its Web site, is ambitious: "To become the best public library in the world by being so tuned in to the people we serve and so supportive of each other's efforts that we are able to provide highly responsive service." For the city, the new library has also achieved an additional unexpected bonus: new tourism revenue. In fact, a 1 percent increase in tourism will yield $1 billion in new economic activity statewide over the next twenty-five years.

Voters supported the new library, through a landmark "Libraries for All" bond measure that garnered a whopping 69 percent approval rating at the polls. It's no surprise it passed with such a high margin, according to Rahaim. He informs me that Seattle is the most well-educated city in the United States. According to the 2000 Census data, 53.6 percent of adults have college degrees, and many of them use the library as their central information space.

Brains attract brawn

With such an educated workforce, it's no wonder so many corporations call Seattle home. The triumvirate of Microsoft, Amazon, and Starbucks is impressive enough. Add Nordstrom and Costco to the list and it's an out-and-out showcase of international brands. Rahaim offers up a possible explanation: "People in Seattle want to work hard and have quality of life. Employers here recognize and encourage that ideal." He holds up Starbucks as an example: even their half-time employees get full health benefits.

Once achieving mega-success a corporate mogul may wonder what to do with the wealth. Thus, the master patron—Seattle style—is born. Both founders of Microsoft, Bill Gates and Paul Allen, have taken philanthropy in Seattle to an unprecedented level. The Bill and Melinda Gates Foundation has an active program around the world and in the Pacific Northwest—committing a total of more than $10 billion since its inception. Paul Allen has given away more than $825 million so far and has been named one of the top ten philanthropists in the United States. He's given the people of Seattle such cultural transformations as the Experience Music Project and the Allen Institute for Brain Science. As a landholder of several key parcels in the city's core, Allen is in a position to contribute significantly to Seattle's grand visions for itself.

While philanthropy may come easily for the wealthy, being comfortable with the role may not. As John Bryan, former Sara Lee CEO, observes, "In Seattle, they don't like to think of themselves as classic philanthropists." People like Paul Allen have charted out a new course for giving, as the rules of the Carnegie and Rockefeller–style funding don't sit well with Seattle. In fact, Seattlelites typically shun traditional displays of status. The citizenry's sense of fashion, often a marker of status, is downplayed with fleece and baggy khakis. People I spoke to told me the story of the new wife of a Seattle Mariner who was asked to comment on Seattle's sense of style and quipped that "People in Seattle dress like they're prepared for a hiking emergency." This attitude toward appearances broadcasts rugged self-determination. How fitting for a city where entrepreneurs thrive.

Philanthropy in the twenty-first century is certain to look very different than in the past. There is a greater emphasis on measuring success as a result of funding. Benefactors now take a more comprehensive and systematic approach to charitable giving. This means even philanthropic activity will change forms and innovate as it needs to, in a RenGen city.

Master artists

Master patrons will undoubtedly attract master artists. Seattle is home to many artists, of course, but two artists at the top of their trade live and work in Seattle: Dale Chihuly of Chihuly Art Glass and Rob Schaub of the Seattle Opera Company.

Dale Chihuly is said to have revolutionized the studio glass movement. Sculpting glass since the mid-1960s, he's gone on to garner awards around the world. Chilhuly grew up in Tacoma, Washington, and has stayed true to his roots. He cofounded

Pilchuck School—50 miles north of Seattle—which has become an international gathering place for glass artists. He's also developed legendary studios in Seattle, called simply The Boathouse. To measure the pull that a master artist can have on an area, there are now thirty-five art glass studios in Seattle. It makes Seattle the largest and most concentrated glassblowing city in the world outside of Venice, Italy.

As Chihuly put Seattle on the map for art glass, the Seattle Opera Company has done so for world-class opera. The Seattle Opera Company produces five operas a year with extraordinary success. They built a new home in 2004, McCaw Hall, which opened to flattering reviews, and they've been able to deliver consistent, superior music and staging to the people of Seattle.

As I stand on the stage in McCaw Hall, Bob Schaub, the technical director for the Seattle Opera Company, lets me in on the secrets of the stage floor. The stage boasts a cavernous drop that allows actors to swan dive to their deaths, and hydraulic lifts enable effects like a 60-foot mechanical dragon to stalk the stage and breathe real fire. Schaub came to Seattle after an intense period in Hollywood, working in special effects and scenery design. He fled to Seattle "to cool his heels." Just like an old-fashioned pioneer, he came with no job, few prospects, but a good deal of self-confidence. As he talks, I am dimly aware that the ambitious productions he mounts are beyond the realm of most theatrical companies, especially in a second-tier city. Later that day, as I look over the production photos, I see step-by-step how the fire-breathing dragon came to life. Schaub confesses it was a complicated feat.

"Why do you go to that extreme?" I ask. He gives a hearty laugh. "We do it because it *is* hard. It means if we can do the dragon, we can do lots of other things." He explains further how his team handily tackled the onstage campfire for the witches cauldron in *Macbeth* based on what they had learned from the dragon project.

Robert Schaub has trained an entire cadre of technicians in Seattle. He has upped the ante for the performing arts in the region, and he has been generous in sharing his expertise—which extends all the way to the Seattle Fire Department. Like Donato Bramante, his historical importance will not be his creations, but his commitment to ambitious work. That spirit has been handed down to a generation of designers in Seattle. This, too, tills the soil for Seattle, making it ripe for a renaissance.

In the midst of all these great aspects, what is it finally about Seattle that makes it a RenGen city?

It's the large swath of citizens and civic leaders who are committed to protecting the environment. It's the diversity of physical, emotional, and physiological spaces at multiple scales and levels. It's a determination to preserve the city's authenticity and the catalytic personalities within it. It's a sound infrastructure of art, architecture, and wealth to build upon for the future. It will be up to the city to manage growth effectively—whether physically or philanthropically. But if there were a Seattleite response to that challenge, surely it would be, "Grab your fleece and let's talk about it over coffee . . ."

Providence

A name like Providence makes you think there is something in the cards for this city. Providence, Rhode Island, was, in fact, the birthplace of the American Industrial Revolution, which might make it an unlikely candidate for an urban renaissance. But that historical backdrop—fused with an overlay of business, design, and vintage architecture all tightly packed into a bustling downtown—are all features that give Providence the rejuvenated energy to earn it the full right to its nickname, "The Renaissance City."

We caught up with Peter Bramante, the executive director of the Arts & Business Council of Rhode Island, Inc., to explore the cultural magnetism in Providence. As a remarkable historical note, Peter is actually related to the Renaissance figure Donato Bramante, famous for his design of St. Peter's Basilica in Rome.

An audience for artists

Peter Bramante started his career as a dancer and choreographer. He and two other collaborators moved to Providence from New York; they wanted to form a dance company where they could create original material. In this way, Bramante epitomizes the RenGen ethos. As he says, "The entrepreneurial spirit was very closely tied to artistic process" in that venture. As the company grew, he and his business collaborators watched the city renew itself.

"We built an audience for our artistic work while we built a structure to support and deliver it," he explains. So what is it that attracted Bramante away from New York, the mecca of the U.S. dance world, to Providence, Rhode Island?

The built environment

Back when the United States was still a developing nation, Providence was one of the wealthiest places to live in the

"Independent Man State," as Rhode Island was known. That wealth, combined with a level of tolerance imbued from founder Roger Williams, created a favorable climate for creative activities.

"There's such a strong history for innovation and creativity in Providence," explains Bramante. "Textile and silversmith mills represented a fusion of design and business."

The historic downtown (called Downcity) architecture is intact and authentic in its original design, and you can see it in the fabric of the built (as opposed to natural) environment. Providence was lucky, in that it escaped a lot of the "urban renewal" efforts of the 1960s and '70s. Now Downcity Providence is on the register of historic places.

Bramante paints a picture of exuberance, energy, and unlimited possibilities for Providence. He gives me the impression that he is pulling the former glory of the place into the current day. He puts Providence in a nutshell as he quips, "Now, it's the best of the compact, urban environments—and yet you're ten minutes from one of the best beaches on the East Coast."

A master instigator choreographs a scalable community experience

Providence is quite small, and Rhode Island itself is only 30 by 40 miles. That density provides ample opportunity for people to cross paths and for connections to happen. Bramante reflects on how his own past career influences his work today: "A choreographer arranges space for optimal design and communication. An urban planner uses space to look at the fabric and the aesthetic of an urban area." As Providence's "instigator," he works with urban planners and other arts administrators to integrate how the city works and to create communication spaces.

Bramante describes the community spirit in Providence as "kinetic." That innovation and the freedom to take risks are easier because the barriers are a little lower. Why? He chalks it up to size. People can start small and scale up.

An affordable space for artists

Classic industrial buildings on the West Side of Providence have naturally attracted artists with their low cost and potential for urban lofts. The city recognized this attraction and charted a course to revitalize the buildings. The Rhode Island legislature passed a tax incentive bill that granted up to a 50 percent abatement for developers to renovate these industrial spaces. It has amounted to a $5 billion new investment for the city.

Reutilizing spaces—and seeing whole neighborhoods reclaimed and reused—brings more energy to the city. "You're really seeing whole communities come back to life with this program. It's creating a new economy—and it's really tied to this creative innovation," Bramante explains.

The city has taken proactive steps to keep the population that attracted creativity in the first place, and has set aside 20 percent of the renovated spaces as affordable housing for artists. Artists can afford own their spaces in Providence—AS220 and Groundwerx/Perishable Theatre are good examples. "'In perpetuity' and owning your own space can mean a lot to an artist," laughs Bramante.

Talk about affordable housing: a project in Providence called Monohasset Mill is a textbook case study for the adaptive reuse of an industrial building. Four artists got together to start the project, and now the historic mill complex offers subsidized and below-market rate live/work condos geared specifically for artists. Units are available to working artists who have demonstrated local community involvement and leadership. A gallery/community space in Monohasset Mill helps solidify the West Side as a bona fide arts district.

Not only does the city provide subsidized housing for artists, it also provides free medical care. The Rhode Island Free Clinic was set up because the community values artistic contributions and realizes that artists and small business employees cannot always afford to pay for health insurance.

Citywide events

In addition, Providence hosts major cultural festivals for its size, such as:

Waterfire: a spectacular fire sculpture installation of 100 bonfires on the three rivers in Downcity. In fact, the Waterfire Web site lists it as "a moving symbol of Providence's renaissance."

FirstWorks: really two festivals, one for kids and one for adults. It is described as an international art festival that allows participants of all ages to "Experience the Art of What's New."

Soundsession: an interdisciplinary music festival with a cross-pollination of different cultural influences. More than 60,000 people attended the weeklong event in July 2006.

This makes for a highly animated environment that draws people together and gets them interacting with new art and ideas, as well as each other—all musts for the RenGen to flourish.

Incubator for design to business innovation

RISD (short for the Rhode Island School of Design, and pronounced *riz-dee*) and Bryant University teamed up to create the Center for Design & Business. The Center is an incubator to help graduates and entrepreneurs turn ideas into real businesses. It provides communal resource space, office modules, and professional development opportunities for selected artistic businesses.

They put on a conference each year, called Success By Design. They've brought in major speakers such as Michael Graves, Martha Stewart, and James Dyson to think about how design influences manufacturing. Given Providence's industrial past, it's a way to connect art and design with manufacturing to explore what comes out of the confluence.

Infrastructure changes

The river that cuts through Providence was once paved over with landfill—until Providence initiated spectacular efforts to reclaim it. The result has sparked a renewed interest in Downcity arts and culture.

Providence has put in a foundation for creative spaces in the city and innovative new enterprise. Providence is now working on a project to reconnect the industrial waterfront and Downcity, and in the process will redirect an interstate highway around the city outskirts. That is, they are literally moving the vehicles of individualization (cars) away from the community areas of shared cultural connections.

Town-and-gown collaboration

Brown University, RISD, Providence College, Johnson & Wales University, Roger Williams University—all of these universities, and more, call Providence home. And the students are called on occasionally to contribute their talents to the city.

Bramante tells the story of a university/business/design collaboration—the fusion of opposites so typical for the RenGen. It's a story about the creative inspiration of seemingly opposite people working together to solve an environmental problem.

A few oceanographic researchers from the University of Rhode Island were trying to restore some of the fish habitats in the Providence harbor. To do this, they needed to replant underwater eel grass, which was critical for the fish survival. They tried planting the seeds normally, but the eel grass seeds would not embed properly and the plants kept dying.

Inventively using their connections in the community, the scientists were led to a manufacturer that made the machines that inject jelly into jelly donuts. When the manufacturer heard the scientists' problem, he wondered if his jelly-donut injection machine might be retrofitted to help their cause.

So the scientists and manufacturer went to the arts community in Providence and brought in an industrial designer to tweak the machine's design. The designer retrofitted the jelly donut injection machine onto a sled that could be dragged along the bottom of the bay. As the revised machine slid along, it would inject eel grass seeds into the muddy bottom of the bay—much like it injected jelly into jelly donuts.

And sure enough, the seeds embedded, the eel grass grew, and the fish returned. It was made possible because representatives from completely different fields—manufacturing, design, and science—could find each other and ingeniously collaborate to solve a specific problem.

That sums up the essence of Providence: collaboration that brings forth organic rejuvenation by investing in aesthetic design and reuse in a small space.

Philadelphia

Beloved by Ben Franklin and many who followed, Philadelphia is the home of some of the earliest history in America. But it also has one of liveliest creative cultures in the United States. With its stately architecture as a backdrop, Philadelphia's vibrant art, music, and intellectual scene hums with RenGen energy. The decade from 1995 to 2004 was one of explosive growth for arts, cultural, and humanities organizations in Greater Philadelphia. The number of arts organizations almost doubled—from 523 to 999.

Leading the growth is Peggy Amsterdam, president of the Greater Philadelphia Cultural Alliance. As a native Philadelphian, she's served as the city's unofficial "Master Instigator" who has, piece by piece, transformed the city into a RenGen haven.

Amsterdam keeps a frantic schedule. Since 2000, she has directed the Alliance, which has become the region's premier leadership and advocacy organization for arts and culture. Amsterdam has brought together more than 300 organizations that collaborate to make up the Cultural Alliance.

Collaboration for culture

Early in her tenure, Amsterdam launched an ambitious city-wide "Campaign for Culture" as a broad umbrella advocacy campaign for arts and culture. The goals of the effort were to stimulate positive public awareness of arts and culture, to increase attendance at Greater Philadelphia cultural institutions, and to develop marketing capacity at nonprofit arts and culture organizations.

One such "Campaign for Culture" event is the Center City Arts & Culture Week. Every October since 2004, the top cultural organizations in the city declare a week in which venues such as the Kimmel Center, the Opera Company of Philadelphia, and the Pennsylvania Academy of Fine Arts offer half-price tickets and many free events for residents to explore all that the city has to offer. It is precisely this mixing—making high-brow art available to middle and low-income people—that has fostered such a palpable sense of energy in Philly.

An outgrowth of the Campaign for Culture was the online entertainment Philly Fun Guide. It was programmed to help people take advantage of their leisure time more consistently. In Amsterdam's words, "It's how we got the doers to do more." Part marketing effort, part awareness-raising, and part professional development-effort, Campaign for Culture was deemed so successful that is received a $2 million grant by the Pew Charitable Trust for marketing programs from 2005 to 2007.

The collaborative spirit has led to a variety of initiatives that have amped up the energy level in Philly. A *National Geographic* article reports,

> *On the first Friday of every month, the art galleries of the Old City—a dense cluster of nineteenth-century buildings near the Delaware River—throw open their doors to all comers. This has created an effervescent social scene, helping to jump-start the revival of the Old City. Now, arguably, it's the liveliest urban neighborhood between SoHo in New York and SoBe in Miami. The area has more students—some 290,000—than Boston, making Philadelphia a bona fide playground for the young.*

Funding for creative activities: Master patrons on board

The Pew grant money didn't come out of nowhere. Philly has a strong history of funding the arts, through programs such as the five-county Arts Fund. To date, the five-county fund has given away more than $1.17 million to more than 539 artists and art organizations in the area.

Sometimes, though, RenGen movers-and-shakers need more than encouragement. They need desks, chairs, and places in which to work. Luckily, the Arts & Business Council of Greater Philadelphia has seen this need and met it with the Resources Bank. Sponsored by Sunoco, the Resources Bank distributes used office furniture and equipment from the business community to arts and cultural organizations, and has donated $1 million worth of materials so far. In the Philadelphia suburb of Norristown, officials have even offered incentives such as tax breaks and grants to bring artists in.

Apprenticeship programs make a comeback

As the fictional South Philadelphia hero Rocky Balboa once told an opponent: "You fight great, but I'm a great fighter." He became a great fighter because he had a good coach. And today, Philadelphia's youth have more access to mentorship and apprenticeship programs. For example, the Walnut Street Theatre in Philadelphia offers a professional apprenticeship program as a training ground for young theatre hopefuls. Applications are accepted for carpentry, casting, costumes, stage crew, props, scene painting—and more—in addition to acting. The program is a full-time commitment that lasts anywhere from six to eleven months. During the program, the students receive medical insurance, gym membership, and access to a broad range of classes, as well as defined objectives for the duration of their stay.

The Fabric Workshop and Museum offers apprenticeship training programs for high school, college, and postgraduate students. The students learn all aspects of fabric silk-screen printing. Over a twelve-week period, the program develops both artistic and industrial skills for the fabric and textile industry.

The Philadelphia Furniture & Furnishings Show offers an Apprenticeship Forum, in which would-be apprentices post requests for mentors in specific disciplines, such as furniture design and ceramics.

Apprenticeships are not limited to the arts, of course. Trades such as cabinetmaking, welding, and plastering are omnipresent with local labor unions. The Naval Surface Warfare Center in Philadelphia also has a program to introduce local students to science and engineering through the Science and Engineering Apprentice Program (SEAP). Designed for high school students, it stimulates students' interest in science and gives them exposure to professional methods for a full eight weeks during the summer.

Knowledge infrastructure and institutions

With its eighty-four colleges, Philadelphia has approximately 290,000 students. Prestigious institutions such as the University of Pennsylvania rub shoulders with other top schools in the area such as Bryn Mawr, Drexel, Swarthmore, Villanova, and Temple.

Some of the most prestigious arts schools in the country are based in Philly: the Art Institute of Philadelphia; the Curtis Institute of Music; the Pennsylvania Academy of the Fine Arts; and the Moore College of Art and Design, which is exclusively for women.

South Philly hosts a ton of affordable arts classes for young students, as well—The Rock School for Dance, Settlement Music School (Curtis Branch), Fleisher Art Memorial (tuition-free!), and Point Breeze Performing Arts Center.

Last but not least, the Free Library of Philadelphia is a jewel of the city. Its fifty-four branches have collections include more than seven million items. A few of the standout RenGen programs include the Regional Foundation Center, where artists can get help with grantwriting and proposals, the world's largest lending library of orchestral performance material (the Fleisher Collection) and the library's lecture series, which attracts luminaries such as Noble laureate Seamus Heaney and Ross King.

Philadelphia reborn

What is it about an old city like Philadelphia that makes it a catalytic center of urban renaissance? It's a unique combination of access to art museums, art schools, and major performing arts venues; a strong sense of collaborative civic awareness; educational infrastructure for students from age five to the Ivy League; and the relative abundance of apprenticeships and guilds for training young talent. Add to that some low-tech assets, like a citywide mural project and very walkable city centers with physical green space where Philadelphians can stroll, relax, and engage their creative imaginations.

Chicago

Chicago is a city where opposites peacefully coexist. Where a smoky blues bar sits right down the street from one of the country's leading art museums. It's a city that can hold both the Sox *and* the Cubs, and where neighborhoods that range from Puerto Rican to Polish live in relative harmony. What is more, these opposites do more than coexist. The diversities and dichotomies of Chicago actually feed into each other, to give rise to an overall creative expression of culture that brings the whole community together. Nowhere is this creative expression of culture more apparent than in Chicago's Loop.

To understand more about the Loop and its impact on the city's RenGen energy, our research team talked with Ty Tabing, the executive director of the Chicago Loop Alliance, a business-improvement district that is focused on making the Loop a destination for Chicagoans and travelers alike.

Tabing's background as the former executive director of the Greater State Street Council and as an assistant commissioner with the City of Chicago's Department of Planning and Development means he combines business savvy with acute political awareness; he is a master organizer for the city. A Midwesterner by birth, Tabing spent time in the nation's capitol working for a congressman before returning to his roots to help reinvigorate the de facto capitol of the Midwest.

The Loop: What it was then

Tabing describes the Loop of yesterday as an empty concrete shell. It's where people worked every day, and emptied every night. He paints a picture of rancid bus fumes, racial tension, and general dismissal of the Loop as anything more than corporate jungle. Out of that decay has emerged a rebirth, with the creation of Millennium Park as the turning point.

Carved from a former railroad graveyard, Millennium Park, as discussed earlier in the book, was the $475-million-dollar cornerstone of Mayor Daley's 1998 plan to revitalize Chicago. The new park connects cultural museums, the Art Institute, and everyday leisure areas with world-class architecture, open-air digital video exhibits, and more. As Tabing attests, "It's 23 acres of green space," right in the heart of Chicago. He compares it to Central Park in New York, and notes that residential addresses close to the park have become the most desirable in the city.

It's also the fastest-growing segment in terms of construction. "There are cranes all over the place here," he says. People are moving in from the suburbs for the "urban dweller" experience.

As Tabing describes how they've counted the number of canopies, invested in wheelchair-accessible curb cuts, and increased the amount of niches for people to duck under if it starts to rain, it becomes apparent that Chicago has made a serious commitment to the pedestrian experience. Tabing notes that the Palmer House, the grande dame of downtown Chicago hotels, has committed $150 million in renovation funds, largely on the strength of the Loop's growing status as a destination locale.

Residential life in the Loop

But turning a workplace jungle into a dynamic, changeable urban playground he calls "mixed use development" doesn't come overnight. Tabing reminds me that residents need grocery stores, places to walk their dogs, and places to socialize. The old stereotype of the Magnificent Mile of shopping gives way to an "edutainment" space that maintains the authenticity of the neighborhood—complete with a farmer's market—and encourages the free flow of creative expression.

It's more than museums

The residential neighborhood shares space with cultural institutions. After all, Chicago is home to The Art Institute, the Martin D'Arcy Museum of Art, the Museum of Contemporary Art, the Field Museum, the Chicago Children's Museum, Museum of Science and Industry, Museum of Holography, Hemingway Museum, and many more. Tabing describes a dynamism that surpasses simply displaying art or artifacts—it includes a theatre district, an educational anchor, and a vibrancy that comes from people interacting on the streets themselves.

About twenty-five years ago, Chicago nurtured a nascent theatre scene. By the time the city grew up, it had spawned the likes of John Malkovich, Gary Sinise, Joan Allen, Laurie Metcalf, David Mamet, Mary Zimmerman, and David Schwimmer. There are plenty more. The League of Chicago Theatres helped the scene along; it now boasts more than 170 member theaters that banded together to better promote and support theater in Chicago. A HotTix booth—second in revenues only to New York's TKTS program among theatre discount organizations—helps connect people with live performances. And the League's efforts have paid off handsomely. The City Council passed a resolution in 2004 that declares Thursdays as "Theater Thursdays," in which younger audiences can see a live performance at a deep discount.

Another youth-oriented street event is the Street Beat on State Street. It coincides with "Fashion Focus Chicago" in September, as the city rolls out red carpet and risers on the street itself. Elite models display the latest creations from the next generation of designers. "It makes for a funky juxtaposition," says Tabing. "It's a good balance between planned events and the ephemeral nature of the street." The weeklong Fashion Focus events include the Gen Art Shop CHICago and a host of other programs that call attention to up-and-coming fashion designers who work and live in Chicago.

Looptopia is another all-city event scheduled for May 2007. It's planned to be an all-night party with parades, fireworks, and live performances to rival the "White Nights" festival in Paris. Murals and downloadable Loop audiotours will drive interest and awareness for Looptopia, as the city celebrates its latest neighborhood.

In addition to Taste of Chicago, Art Chicago, or the Chicago Blues Festival, there are smaller, more boutique festivals in the Loop. "We host one on Memorial Day called the International Male Leather Competition," Tabing says. "IML for short." And there's the Great Chicago Places and Spaces Event, which celebrates the notable architecture of the City.

A home to great architecture

With that, our conversation turns to architecture, as Chicago has been home or inspiration to more than its share of famous architects—the Prairie School and Frank Lloyd Wright being the best known. Of course, Chicago has also been an inspiration of modernist architects and furniture designers, such as Daniel Burnham, Mies van der Rohe, and contemporaries such as Rem Koolhaas and Frank Gehry.

Tabing speculates that the city inspires great spatial thinking around the built environment because there's no topography. "It's so flat," he jokes, "there are no mountains for people to look at." The architecture is something that gives the Chicago environment a distinct sense of creative possibility.

Education, students, and lifelong learning

The lack of mountains has not deterred many 18 to 24 year-olds from coming to Chicago. Besides notable Chicago universities such as Northwestern and the University of Chicago, other institutions attract approximately 55,000 students to the Loop itself every week. More than twenty higher education institutions—The Art Institute, Columbia College, and DePaul being three of the most well known—all foster a sense of revitalized youth culture centered on art and design. Taken together, it effectively makes the Loop the "largest college town in Illinois" and generates $777 million in direct and indirect economic activity, according to an Impact Study done in January 2005 on Higher Education in the Loop.

Of course, youth are not the only Chicagoans who are serious about learning in the Loop. The newly remodeled Harold Washington Library sits at the corner of State Street and Congress Parkway. As the central campus of Chicago Public Library's seventy-nine branches, it features 450 multipurpose meeting rooms, 385 auditoriums, 60 classrooms, and 63 video theaters—not to mention the vast breadth of materials on more than 70 miles of shelving.

Understandably, the central library is a magnet for Chicago's expressives and the city government knows it. At a recent library technology conference, Mayor Daley described Chicago's libraries as "the heartbeat of the community."

In support of that heartbeat, the city has built thirty-two full-service neighborhood libraries since 1995, with fourteen more being developed. They've also invested heavily in technology with free WiFi and downloadable eResources, such as audiobooks. As Library Commissioner Mary A. Dempsey explained, "We treat our Web site as the eightieth branch."

Hallmark of a renaissance

Finally, Chicago embodies ones of the classic characteristics of a renaissance city: access to travel. In the Italian renaissance, this was access by water. In today's culture, it means a major hub of the airline industry. Chicago's O'Hare airport is the busiest in the world. When the city was recruiting Boeing to relocate to Chicago, O'Hare's easy access to Shanghai and Sydney was a critical factor in the city's successful bid.

Chicago embodies one of the boldest campaigns for culture in any American city. One former resident declared that Chicago's success can be credited to a high-concept cosmopolitanism with a healthy dose of Midwestern pragmatism. Now that embodies the RenGen concept of fusion.

What is it that makes these four specific cities—Seattle, Providence, Philadelphia, and Chicago—centers for the RenGen? We outlined the major factors up front, but what most struck our research team was a palpable *sense of the possible* that each of these cities possessed. These cities each came up with creative ways to improve the lives of their citizenry. They each (in their own way) put structures in place to make their cities extraordinary by design—be it tax abatements, a reclaimed core of urban architecture, plenty of outdoor green spaces, live theater, or the relative profusion of educational opportunities in the form of colleges, universities, and libraries.

Seattle, Providence, Philadelphia, and Chicago all have a mojo that encourages broad mixing of culture and people in an authentic experience that rings true. They count among their citizenry master artists and master patrons, who take personal pride in making contributions that give off an energy of connectedness. These places reverberate with RenGen energy.

CHAPTER THIRTEEN

What Will Rule in a RenGen?

This book is a signal flag being vigorously waved in your direction. We are in an interim period when the sensate civilization is collapsing and a new ideological age is rising to replace it. It is the end of the end, and the beginning of the beginning. It is a messy place, this rising new renaissance, fraught with inconsistencies and paradoxes. Things fused for today's purposes will fall asunder tomorrow with the next technological advance. This is the RenGen.

At this point, you probably want some clear answers about what to expect. Well, here they are.

Thriving in the RenGen will depend on how well you react to three immutable preconditions of a renaissance:

1. Death comes first
2. The presence of a facilitating medium
3. The rise of the Beautiful Mind

Let's consider these in turn.

Death Comes First

As a society declines, it becomes more polarized as factions stake out turf they can cling to. Here, you have a choice. You can either embrace the widening middle ground now opening up between the polarities or exploit the passions on the extremes. Organizations that follow the latter course will look and feel more traditional and be able to cash in on the loyalty of a fervent customer base. The problem is that this direction has a short life span: it is not where the society is headed over the next twenty to thirty years. RenGenners can be found in the middle ground. But hitching your star to the RenGen movement means committing to innovation. As you consider taking the leap, you now know that what you'll encounter is a widespread redefinition of who we are, what we believe, and how we see the world. So, expect to experiment as a matter of course. Once you develop an approach to experimentation, you will enter a cycle of innovation that is essential to becoming a successful RenGen company.

An important caveat about innovation is that it has a price. The type of brainpower it takes to support the invention process is staggering, and the upheaval these changes can generate within an organization is considerable. But organizations of any size that lack a commitment to research and development will risk irrelevance in the RenGen. As sobering as that is, keep in mind that a renaissance is not a revolution; rather, it builds upon what worked best in earlier times while adding fresh ideas born of a new mind-set. Don't expect that you'll have to scrap everything and start over and over again. Instead, you will be focused more than ever on your core strengths, but will be deploying them in imaginative new ways.

You will innovate by adding, subtracting, and rearranging components, using Collage Theory to create something new and compelling. Because this is not a linear process, you and your team must create a structure for experimentation, deciding when to move the pieces, and why—based on your own business priorities—and determining what you must add to the picture to appeal to the RenGen mind set.

A Facilitating Medium

The Internet will facilitate the second renaissance. Indeed, it's already doing so. But, like other tools, it has inherent limitations. For instance, many people find it difficult to conceive the Internet as a tool to address complex social issues that require human reasoning. Our task here is not to foreclose on the technology's potential, but to discover its boundaries by harnessing it to solve important problems.

Consider Justine Cassell, a professor of communications studies and computer science at Northwestern University who developed the Embodied Conversational Agent, a virtual human capable of interacting with humans using both language and nonverbal behavior. Cassell has investigated the role this technology can play in children's lives; her Story Listening System is a companion technology that facilitates peer support for learning language skills. She has also used linguistic and psychological analyses to look at the effects of online conversation on self-esteem, self-determination, and sense of community among a diverse group of young people.

This may be the ultimate fusion the RenGen delivers. As Cassell sees it, once machines have human-like capabilities—meaning they are sensitive as well as intelligent—they can be used to evoke from humans the most human and humane of our capabilities. This fusion of analog and digital challenges the premise that our lives are automatically improved by technology—unless we can imbue machines with the best of what is *human*.

The Internet will also distribute extraordinary creative output. It is so fertile a medium, in fact, that it is hard to imagine where the limits will be set. Perhaps we will decide that individually. When our imaginations are sated, we may dip in and out of the creative current funneled by the Web as we need to. Or perhaps the flow of ideas and information will all keep gushing forth and we will attune ourselves to it until it becomes simply a vivid backdrop. Either way, while the mega audiences participating in online social networking and consumer-created content may be transient phenomena, they represent deeper cultural forces that are not going away. Experiment with varieties of online content, or risk oblivion.

The Rise of the Beautiful Mind

Organizations that will rule in the RenGen will know how to find potential inspiration for new ground. They will master the PING process. This goes beyond brainstorming and focus groups to involve genuine discovery and active problem-solving. This can be as elaborate as planning a learning experience involving customers or as simple as a conference call enabling customers who have been sent the storyboard of the problem or the prototype to offer their own ideas. Organizations will establish "artists in residence" programs. Hired brains will replace hired hands as companies recruit ringers to PING with their teams.

Help stock peoples' storehouse of knowledge

Building people's storehouse of knowledge will open up an array of new business opportunities. Look around. Identify your educational assets and exploit them. This can simply mean giving your customers access to bright people who come through your company.

I recently moderated an event with Jack Welch, the legendary CEO of General Electric. One business owner in the audience was a defense contractor who had invited military brass to take in the experience. When we opened for questions, an admiral asked for advice on how to motivate people in high-stakes situations when there are none of the usual incentives, such as monetary reward or fear of being fired. Mr. Welch scratched his head, acknowledged the challenge the admiral faced, and did his best to answer the question. Everyone learned something that day about the human complexity involved in managing the armed forces. And the business owner who had thought enough to invite his customers to an executive learning event was the biggest winner. Helping people learn will be critical in the RenGen.

Creative thinking will flourish

The creative aspect of the beautiful mind has an urgency to it. Perhaps that is because the work that lies ahead to mend— and defend—the planet will be so demanding. But people seem driven to establish their identities by flexing their creative muscles. Among the benefits of using their creative talents, people described a liberating feeling associated with working in a creative mode. So, being creative helps people find themselves and feel good—two important ingredients for any trend to last.

If this flourishing of creativity and ideas has the same effects on contemporary society as it did on fourteenth-century Europe, we can expect more and more talented people in all disciplines yielding a vast range of innovations. The rising social importance of learning and understanding the world around us—whether conscious or instinctive—reinforces the fact that, cognitively, we are gearing up for the renaissance.

What Your Organization Must Grasp

So now, you have the big concepts under your belt. To make those concepts more meaningful, here are seven touch points that successful RenGen organizations must grasp.

1. Fusion, not fission

If the twentieth century fractured the personality through endless choices for defining who we are, the twenty-first century moves the other way. Fusion means more integration. Ironically, while we strive to give consumers choice and control, we also make their lives unmanageable. People can handle only so many issues and identities until they have to discard something to gain something new. Making consumers feel they are in control is critical, but the companies/organizations that will dominate in the RenGen will be those that also help consumers resolve the dissonance created when they must choose between equally attractive options. Even services that help people sort and select suitable elements to fuse on their own will be valued. What's at stake for people in a fusing world is the assembly of the self. In his book *TechGnosis*, Erik Davis describes the convergence of informatics with spirituality. For example, Davis explains the self as a vessel shaped by the practices we engage in: arts, diet, sex, dance, learning, sport, contemplation, friendship, ethics. The Internet is a technology that has allowed us to move beyond the simple automation of tasks to a more abstract state where the self finds expression by assembling its own meaning. As our choices in life increase, our fragmented identities are the raw material for the creative integration of the self. This is not mutation of the self, but transmutation, and it is very RenGen.

Fusion is an application of Collage Theory. Even in the creative process, merging a winning "classic" with a new feature that might not otherwise go with it can prove to be a launch pad for new ideas. I recently received an invitation for a "Blue Jeans and Bling" event that was a fusion between a fancy ball and a barbecue. The invitation said I could expect steaks on the grill, a country swing band, and a hay bale to share with my date. Attire? Denim and diamonds of course.

2. An open-ended process trips the trigger

A RenGen vision that rings true demands original ideas. So, how will you make sure that what you embrace will stimulate those ideas? The answer is to let your people contribute theirs. To do that you must create room for their engagement. Starbucks conceives programs, like Make Your Mark, that are intentionally open-ended enough for employees and customers to jump in and contribute their creativity.

The Web is endlessly open-ended, inviting people's imaginations to come out and play. Consider the case of the 3-D virtual world called Second Life, entirely built and owned by its residents. Since opening to the public in 2003, it has grown explosively with virtual residents from around the globe. The owners of Second Life describe it as a "Digital continent, teeming with people, entertainment, experiences, and opportunity. Once you've explored a bit, perhaps you'll find a perfect parcel of land on which to build your house or business." At the time of this writing, the venerable advertising agency Leo Burnett had snapped up a 16-acre parcel for its employees to develop, swap ideas, and gather around a virtual water cooler. Second Life built the setting for an open-ended world; the rest is limited only by the creativity of its residents.

3. Individuals make a collective difference

RenGen people believe they can make a difference. Expect to be confronted with ideals that up to now had little to do with your competitive edge. Principles such as advancing the greater good, advocacy, environmentalism, tolerance, and inclusion will be sacrosanct in the RenGen. Those organizations with the vision to address these values in ways that are genuinely meaningful will galvanize their work cultures and bond with their customers.

Pitirim Sorokin posited the theory that civilizations eventually decline because the conditions that bring them about eventually evolve toward irrelevance. In other words, things change enough to create the need for new systems of social organization. He predicted the rise of a society based more on ideals. This idealism gives rise to all forms of new customs and behaviors, chief among them the belief that individuals can make a difference in shaping the new civilization. We need look no further than a shattered New Orleans in Hurricane Katrina's aftermath to find examples of people, especially young people, contributing time and talent to make a difference. When Katrina struck, its force shook the city's social order to its core. Systems failed. Tens of thousands of people suffered, starved, and struggled to survive. In this, chaos, a group of young people formed Emergency Communities to provide pop-up soup kitchens to feed the hungry. All the food is prepared by hand using fresh ingredients, cooked under tented structures that can be swiftly assembled by a few volunteers.

Word of the Emergency Communities spread virally via the Internet as volunteers recruited their friends to join the effort. Here is a description of the experience by Valesa Higman, who shared her journal with her alma mater's alumni magazine, the *Lewis and Clark College Chronicle*:

> My fingers are mosquito bitten. It is a collage of faces, stories, the smell of rotten potatoes, and flies in my face. It is sweat between my shoulder blades, and the first time someone broke down crying in my arms. It is the sweetest thanks I ever received—a rose painted on the back of a book from Ravalee of Waveland, who lost everything in the storm except her paints and a few brushes. It grabbed me from the start, the feeling that I could plunge my hands into a tub of dishwater and help a thousand people. I could chop carrots or peel garlic and make an old man sigh in relief.

The model has proven to be sustainable; one year after its founding, Emergency Communities had expanded to serve a necklace of communities struggling to recover along the Gulf Coast. The nonprofit is recognized and financially supported by the United Way and by more than twenty companies providing cash and in-kind support.

This generation will be much less motivated by traditional incentives. The chance to contribute personal effort toward the greater good will not only be cherished, it will be as routine as taking time off work for vacations or medical leave. Companies who honor it—not to mention facilitate it through their own philanthropy—will rule in the RenGen.

4. Help Wanted: Collaborators for high performance projects

Searching for experienced people to work alongside the design team. We expect every applicant to have excellent PC skills, be confident, outgoing and know their business! You must be commercially minded, have some sales experience and a great personal manner. Enthusiasm and flexibility are essential. An interest in art & design welcomed. *[Excerpted from the job board of a start-up manufacturing company specializing in alternative energy household appliances.]*

For years, management guru Tom Peters evangelized about training people to attack all work as a series of projects. The RenGen will realize that destiny. Project work will not only be the norm, it will become its own discipline. And the ability to deftly define problems so as to embark on the right projects, will become an essential skill. People good at defining problems will rule in the RenGen. Project management will be taught in cross-disciplinary courses on college campuses. User-friendly, intuitive project management technologies will find broader markets. Followed close behind by those who are good at defining problems will be those who collaborate gracefully and still turn out exceptional results.

These developments pose challenges in the workplace. The dot-com era left the debris of many unfinished human experiments in its wake, and the unresolved contention between creatives and engineers was one of them. Still, the complexity of our situation—our reliance on high-tech skills, multiple languages, and rapid analytics—implies the need for many minds to learn to play as a team. "Personability"—that quality that allows people to critique and be critiqued constructively—will be the ruling business etiquette of the RenGen. Easily wounded spirits will be relegated to the sidelines.

5. Leadership's new look

It's no secret that the knowledge society has ignited a redistribution of power away from hierarchies and toward decentralization and self-reliance. Many of the most powerful vectors for societal change will come from fields other than the political arena. Furthermore, new types of players will take the political stage. Though many people scoff at the arrival of Hollywood actors on the political scene—a bipartisan phenomenon—this trend will expand to add new creative voices to the ranks of leadership. Artists, writers, scientists, and entrepreneurs will fill out the field of likely candidates.

Again, this is not so much a revolution as it is a return to our roots. The authors of the Constitution ran businesses and farms, but they were also the country's greatest scholarly talents. Jefferson, Franklin, and Adams all wrote, read, drew maps, invented, and engaged in far-reaching debates about America's future. Look for a renaissance in leadership that will be a juiced-up version of what shaped our country in the eighteenth century.

Women will also complete a cycle of empowerment in the RenGen. The rise of the female is a common theme in world literature that accompanies major societal shifts. According to some theorists, the ascent of women into positions of power coincides with periods of decay, ostensibly to hasten the arrival of a more fertile cycle.

Gwynn Cassidy, the young woman who spearheaded the REAL Hot 100 and whom you met in Chapter 10, is a preview of coming attractions. Inevitably, women will expand their repertoire of roles as part of the distributed model of power, particularly in the area of communications. Advertising, media, entertainment, and publishing will all see more women move to the top. Women also will be active in the sciences, influencing areas like educational technologies, and will accelerate much-needed social change toward distributed rather than hierarchical leadership models.

6. Tapping into roots

In an age of uncertainty, people seek a foundation. Those who provide it in a thoughtful, original way will rule. You don't have to look back much further than the Beatles to tap into the iconography people cling to. On a practical level, most organizations find they must speak to three generations and remain relevant to all of them. Fortunately, all ages derive meaning from the lush library of icons and artifacts contained in our collective consciousness.

Our rapid adoption of the virtual world of the Internet has actually laid the groundwork for the return to roots. This is what Foucault called "technologies of the self"—those automated practices that produce personal identity. The Internet is a veritable supermarket of images and news from other cultures from which we can select and try things on. We deftly mix and remix our identities to the point that a void has opened up inside us.

After all, who are we, really? What can we say about ourselves that is forever true?

To answer that, we must turn to our roots: Irish, Italian, Native American, Polish, Egyptian. . . . And then we are the people our parents raised: Jews, Christians, Muslims. . . . What is especially American is that our ethnicity and religious beliefs are granted plenty of emotional space to coexist with other attributes and still be accepted. This allows us to borrow from the broader civilization when we feel untethered, so the iconography of an ancient religion suddenly holds great appeal.

This need to return to our roots has found expression in things that evoke mysticism, such as incense, colors, and imagery evocative of temples. Take care, though, in employing these icons. Make sure people will give you permission to invoke the traditions they hold dear. Christmas is a prime example of abused iconography that has resulted in a turned-off consumer base.

7. Make mine authentic

The need to surround oneself with objects and habitats that feel authentic springs from the exaltation of roots. People want things that are "real," not prefabricated and mass-produced. It can be tricky to automatically know what might be accepted as "authentic" when your job is to produce something that a large number of buyers need and want.

The RenGen aesthetic dictates preferences for something that feels more real than perfect, something whose form and function make it handsomely useful, something that engages the senses and provides a point of departure for people's imaginations, something that has a story. These features determine what is authentic. The products that embody them will be objects of desire in the RenGen.

The Convergence Culture

In writing this book, I encountered people who wondered if they have a place in the RenGen. They don't want to be left out. They needn't fret. The converging culture, as I have tried to demonstrate in this book, is more inclusive than exclusive. It presents countless opportunities. It is a collage, not a hierarchy. The lifestyle pursuits that once were a matter of social class are being embraced by an ever-expanding segment of the population. As this dissolves the barriers between social classes, experts anticipate a new social order that is a multifaceted stratification. As the RenGen society takes shape, people can enjoy the equivalent of academic freedom, freely choosing to listen to hip-hop, earn a second degree, attend a gallery opening, or rent martial arts movies.

Daniel Beaty is the poster child for RenGen theory. Beaty is a rising star who performs one-man shows of original poetry based on the history of the African American experience. "I am hip hop, but I am also opera. I am Ivy League, but I am also 'hood,'" he explained in an interview with the *New York Times*. Beaty looks to be in his late twenties. He earned a degree from Yale and a scholarship to the Aspen Opera Theater, and is a national champion poetry slammer. This freedom, embodied by Beaty, to graze across fields for inspiration has a profound significance throughout our society. It means that people like George Lucas are free to create *Edutopia*, a magazine for teachers. Actor John Lithgow can develop a reading series for schoolchildren. Susan Sarandon and Bono can wield political influence, and Al Gore can become a movie star. Personal authority may be falling away, but it is being replaced by an imperative for personal expression.

Although my analysis of social trends revealed both convergence and divergence—fusion and polarity held in creative tension—the overall patterns point to an emerging confluence. Does convergence of trends mean we face a common destiny? With respect to trends so strong that they change the way we think and act over a period of thirty years, the answer is yes. However, with respect to the individual responses those trends elicit, the answer is no. Mass convergence does not dictate a uniform future because we know individuals adapt to phenomena in unique ways. Each mind and heart synthesizes the impressions taken in to create personal meaning.

The theory of the RenGen is that we reframe the way we see ourselves as actors in the world. Rather than passive consumers, we are contributors. This confidence that we have the potential to contribute something worthy shapes the common culture. We face a time marked by the outpouring of people's interpretations of their world—not just artists, but ordinary people. Who would have known that self-generated media like MySpace.com would tap a vein as rich as 100 million accounts (as of this writing), with users posting their profiles, ideas, poems, hobbies, rants, and riffs? Who could have guessed that thousands of people would quietly take up painting, drawing, dance classes, and writing. My lawyer, for example, has penned three novels and one play. These activities are expressions of our imaginations preparing to go to work to rebuild a civilization facing problems of staggering proportions.

Our changing mind-set also signals a time when compassion and negotiation will serve as social tools to navigate the upheavals of a changing world. I am reminded of a story told to me by David Sedaris, whom I eventually interviewed as part of my research. If you recall, he is the author whose popularity got me PINGing to write this book in the first place.

I asked Sedaris, who was on a book tour, why he thought he was so popular. He expressed amazement that people—all kinds of people—would wait up to six hours in line to get their books signed. Despite his haggard, road-weary look, Sedaris was funny, with a quirky sort of charm. For example, when I asked him how he was holding up, this being his fifteenth stop in as many days, he answered with this story: In one town, after many hours of signing books, a man approached the table Sedaris sat behind and flopped his hand down on it. It was no ordinary hand, Sedaris said. It was a tiny, shrunken hand that would fit a 5-year-old. Sedaris looked up and into the man's eyes, making sure they were connecting. "Wow, that's a really tiny hand," Sedaris chirped. The man gave a weak smile. "Yes, it is," he replied. Sedaris took his time to write a very specific message in the man's book. The man read it, beamed up at Sedaris and said, "Thank you . . . thank you."

That story sticks with me. Who hasn't felt inadequate at some point—underdressed, ill equipped, or just uncomfortable in our own skin? Yet, if a renaissance sees a blossoming of humanity, it means we will take small powers into our hands to inspire others with simple gestures of compassion. Imagine that.

The persistence of change in our lives has made us suspicious of the future. The complexity of life and the speed at which we live it has left many feeling like life is about managing the chaos.

But it is just as plausible to see the various pieces as a collage. If there is an overarching theme I'd like to leave you with it is that what lies ahead is not an abyss, but a renaissance. It may not endure for as long as the 200 years of the European Renaissance, because we live life at such an accelerated pace. So, take a deep breath. Steady yourself. And step out of the mist into an enlightened age of opportunity.

The RenGen at a Glance

Its Metaphysical Basis
▶ Humans and the natural world are interdependent; the fate of one controls the destiny of the other.
▶ Human purpose is interwoven by universal oneness.

Its World View
▶ The world's natural resources are devolving and finite.

Its View of Time and Space
▶ We have preassigned the limits of time and space, but they are not inherently structured as we perceive them.

Its Spiritual Values
▶ What can be imagined can be manifested.
▶ Spirit can be brought into everyday life, work, and physical surroundings.
▶ Heaven is the uplifted state of consciousness—the wonderful, peaceful sense of universal oneness.

Its Moral Code of Action
▶ Transformation of society and the planet can be achieved through modest, personal, constructive acts.
▶ Balance the health of the mind, body, and spirit for true well-being.
▶ Overcome hierarchies that prevent understanding and connectedness.
▶ Return to what is simple, natural, and direct.
▶ Value sensory experience above expert opinion.
▶ Do what you love; love what you do.
▶ Contribute effort toward achieving greater ends.

Its Attitude Toward the Physical Realm
▶ Show a preference for natural processes.
▶ Accept imperfection.
▶ Objects are associative—beloved, they tell a story and convey a sense of belonging.

A Renaissance Timeline

1291	End of the Crusades
1296	Building of Florence Cathedral—"the Duomo"—begins
1300	Temporary end of European slave trade
1313	Gunpowder invented
1327	The Aztecs establish Mexico City
1332	Bubonic plague originates in India
1337	Edward III of England is succeeded by Richard II
1337	Start of the Hundred Years' War between England and France
1348	"Black Death" reaches Europe
1348–51	Seventy-five million people die of the bubonic plague or "Black Death"
1349	Persecution of the Jews in Germany
1369	Building begins on the Bastille in Paris
1378	Great Schism divides the Catholic Church between Rome and Avignon as two popes are elected
1381	Peasants' Revolt in England over unfair taxation
1386	Heidelberg University founded in Germany
1408	Cardinals meet to end the Great Schism

1431	French Catholic heroine Joan of Arc burned at the stake by the English during the Hundred Years' War
1431	Henry VI of England crowned king of France in Paris
1434	Cosimo de'Medici becomes unofficial head of the government of Florence
1440s	Johann Gutenberg develops the printing press
c. 1450	Gutenberg prints the first Bible
1455–1485	War of the Roses fought between the royal families of York and Lancaster for the English throne
1479	Spanish Inquisition targets Jews and Muslims
1483	Richard III crowned King of England
1492	Christopher Columbus reaches the West Indies
1497–1498	Vasco da Gama completes first ocean voyage from Europe to Asia, opening up European trade and colonization of the Far East
1517	Martin Luther launches protest against Roman Catholic Church, marking the beginning of the Protestant Reformation
1519	Charles V becomes Holy Roman Emperor, ruling Germany, Austria, and parts of southeastern Europe
1531	The Medici made Dukes of Florence by Charles V
1534	Act of Supremacy: Henry VIII declares himself head of the Church of England
1543	Copernicus publishes his theory that the earth and planets revolve around the sun
1545–1563	Council of Trent meets; beginning of the Catholic Counter-Reformation

1558–1603	Reign of Elizabeth I of England
1575	The Medici pronounced Grand Dukes of Tuscany by Maximilian II
1577–1580	Sir Francis Drake circumnavigates the world
1588	Spanish Armada is sent by Philip II of Spain to invade England but is defeated
1602	Dutch East India Company founded
1603–1625	James I rules England and Scotland
1609	Galileo constructs the first telescope for use in astronomy
1618–1648	The Thirty Years' War, a series of European conflicts fought mainly in Germany.
1620	The Mayflower lands at Plymouth
1642	Civil War begins in England between Parliamentarians and Royalists
1643–1715	Louis XIV rules France
1649	Charles I of England executed; Cromwell names head of new republic

Information from *Lives and Works in the Arts: From the renaissance to the 20th century*, Vol. I (M.E. Sharpe, 1997).

APPENDIX C

Research Report:
Are Marketing Executives Responding to the Rise of the Cultural Consumer?

During the fall of 2005, LitLamp Communications Group and Meaningful Measurement, under the direction of Donna Surges Tatum, Ph.D., conducted a survey of the membership of the Marketing Executives Networking Group (MENG). The organization has nearly 1,500 members from around the world. Membership is strictly limited to professional marketers who meet the following standards:

Members are marketing, sales, or general management executives whose primary focus is marketing. Membership is initiated via colleague and peer referrals. The group is not currently listed publicly, and membership is available only by referral. MENG is comprised of VPs, SVPs, CMOs, COOs, and presidents. Prospective members must meet the following requirements:

1. Minimum base salary (excluding bonuses, options, etc.) of $150,000
2. Hold title of at least vice president or equivalent
3. Expertise is expected to include at least one of the following fields:
   - Marketing
   - Advertising

- Sales management
- Public relations
- Corporate communications
- Investor relations
- Market research
- Direct marketing
- Business development
- Strategic marketing alliances
- Strategic planning
- Corporate marketing planning
- Product management
- General management (in a marketing-driven business)

The Survey and Its Reliability

The survey was e-mailed to all 1,500+ members. Respondents were assured that their responses would be kept confidential and reported only as aggregate data. Sixty-five people returned the survey—a modest response rate, but expected for executives of this caliber. Participants appear to be representative of the overall MENG membership's fields of expertise. The reliability rating for the survey is an excellent 92 percent.

We should keep this in mind as we consider the results of the survey: The sample size was small but representative, which may have something to do with the topic of the study.

One purpose of the survey is to gauge what might be described as the demand for marketing programs that tap into cultural consumers, both with content and connection. On the whole, there is desire to reach the type of demographics the survey asked about, namely youth and women, as well as those consumers who were described as affluent and well educated.

Demographics of respondents

Participants are experienced marketers. One-third have twenty years in the profession and more than 50 percent have between sixteen and thirty years' experience. There is a wide variety of expertise represented; the respondents' principal marketing industry range from consumer packaged goods, technology, entertainment, market research, health care, media, and many others.

Results

What overall story does the research tell us? First, whether or not they consider the youth market important, this elite group of marketers recognizes that online is the best vehicle to reach them. In fact, online is considered very important for all three of these desirable demographic groups.

What is striking is the pattern of heightened interest in media tactics such as the use of online, public relations, and arts and entertainment marketing.

Affluent and well-educated consumers are prime targets

Affluent, well-educated customers are extremely important targets to these marketers. Preferred tactics for reaching this group rest heavily on the Web, public relations, and arts and entertainment. Other tactics, such as television and radio, took a steep drop-off from those top three. There is also agreement that

more consumers qualify as "well educated" the number widely
believed to fall into that group.

Youth

There is significant divergence among this group on importance of the youth market to their campaigns. The bulk of
respondents ranked it as either "very important" or "not at all
important." Even for those who saw the segment as unimportant,
there was agreement that online marketing was the best way to
reach this age group. Next in importance were public relations
and arts and entertainment marketing. Sports marketing fared
poorly as a tactic for reaching youth, as did direct mail, television, and radio. No matter what, if these marketers were going to
spend any money reaching youth, they would spend it online.

Women

Respondents had a high need to reach women consumers.
This is no surprise since women have constituted a core consumer segment for many years. Given the breadth of participation in the study from across industry sectors, we can see that
the influence of women has moved beyond packaged goods and
retail and into areas such as financial services, automotive, and
technology purchases.

There is a broader arsenal of preferred tactics for reaching
women age 35–55. Online, public relations and print are all considered very important. Radio and sports are ranked as not at
all important. Television fares somewhat better. In fact, television and arts and entertainment were nearly equal in importance
as tactics for reaching this critical segment, with arts trending
higher. Sports marketing fell to the very bottom of the preferred

tactics, revealing that this group of elite marketers does not consider it a useful tool in their mix for reaching the female consumer. Underlying the choice of preferred tactics, as with the affluent/well-educated consumer, is the assumption that this segment reads and connects online to get information.

Anticipated Trends

These executives said they want to learn more about how to market both online and through arts and entertainment platforms. While many said they saw these tactics as important or very important for reaching the most important consumer groups, they were less sure about how to implement. Forty-one percent said they used some type of arts and entertainment tie, but used it very infrequently. So, while arts and entertainment are judged very important or extremely important as a tactic for use with the most prized consumer groups, surprisingly few marketers use the tactic with any frequency. This can be the result of several failures. First, there may be a lack of understanding or expertise as to how to implement these programs, especially in view of the years of experience represented in the response pool and the relative ease of implementing more traditional advertising buys. Another possibility is that there are few examples of high-profile programs in the marketplace to emulate. Marketing is a me-too business in some ways.

Education is an issue. These marketing elites want to learn more about how to market online and through arts and entertainment ties. We can anticipate there will be a need for marketing courses on these topics.

There may be other reasons for the infrequent use of arts and entertainment marketing that are worth considering. Our research team wondered if it is a simple case of risk aversion, a topic frequently talked about in marketing and advertising. The question of why marketers are slow to seize competitive advantage when they spot trends is complex, but the two themes that rise to the top are a fear of failure that could result in termination and a failure of imagination. While the survey didn't pose questions in that vein, the data do reveal a gap between demand for marketing programs in arts and entertainment and lack of execution of such programs in these executives' portfolios today.

Specific Questions

Here are responses to questions from the survey.

Question 1: In the current fiscal year, what tactic have you used most often?

TACTIC	PERCENTAGE OF TOTAL
Television	10%
Print	22%
Radio	4%
Direct	18%
Online	35%
Public relations	6%
Sports marketing	2%
Arts & entertainment marketing	1%
Other	2%

More than one third of the MENG respondents stated that they used online tactics most often in the current fiscal year, followed about 20 percent each who used print and direct. The remaining one quarter of respondents divided the tactics used most often between television, public relations, radio, sports marketing, and other—i.e. promotion and event marketing. No one used arts and entertainment marketing as a primary tactic.

Question 2: In the current fiscal year, what other tactics have you used? Mark all that apply.

TACTICS	PERCENTAGE OF TOTAL
Television	27%
Print	47%
Radio	35%
Direct	47%
Online	63%
Public relations	67%
Sports marketing	18%
Arts & entertainment marketing	41%
Other	20%

MENG respondents use a blend of tactics in addition to the one they use most often. About two thirds also utilize public relations and online; nearly half employ print advertising and direct; one third use radio; one quarter buy television advertising; and 20 percent each use sports marketing and other. "Other" includes trade shows, viral, word of mouth, blogs and influencers, promotion and event marketing, video games—console and online, billboards, and via partner. *Note:* Only one of the respondents uses arts and entertainment marketing as a primary tactic, although over 40 percent have it in their plans.

Question 3: In the next fiscal year, which tactic will you want to learn more about?

TACTICS	PERCENTAGE OF TOTAL
Television	2%
Print	6%
Radio	6%
Direct	2%
Online	43%
Public relations	10%
Sports marketing	2%
Arts & entertainment marketing	25%
Other	4%

This group of MENG respondents is most interested in learning more about online tactics (43%). Another one quarter are most curious about arts and entertainment marketing, and 10 percent want to explore public relations. Print and radio draw about 6 percent interest each. The tactics of least interest, in terms of a desire to learn more about them, are television, direct and sports marketing, although traditionally, they are the most heavily funded in most marketing budgets.

Tactics of interest listed under "Other" include viral/word-of-mouth and podcasts. Of course, it makes sense that experienced marketers already have an understanding of the older tactics and have the most interest in learning about newer ones.

Question 4: People interested in things such as independent film, visual art, and live music are a growing segment.

RESPONSE	PERCENTAGE OF TOTAL
Very strongly agree	6%
Strongly agree	25%
Agree	49%
Disagree	18%
Strongly disagree	0%
Very strongly disagree	2%

An overwhelming 80 percent of the MENG respondents agree with the statement.

Question 5: The knowledge economy is creating a more intelligent consumer.

RESPONSE	PERCENTAGE OF TOTAL
Very strongly agree	8%
Strongly agree	31%
Agree	47%
Disagree	10%
Strongly disagree	2%
Very strongly disagree	2%

These experts also overwhelmingly agree (86%) that the consumer is becoming more intelligent.

Conclusions

Several conclusions can be drawn from the results of this survey of marketing executives.

Affluent, well-educated consumers are key to all industry segments, and respondents believe they will best be reached through nontraditional media.

Those marketers who see youth as an important target will need to crack online information behaviors of this segment or fail. Since the technology shifts and this segment is prone to migrate from one online activity to another, continuing education is important for marketers in this category. It also suggests that specialties will niche around youth marketing as the number of technologies and new media proliferate and this segment adopts them.

There is a clear separation between old and new. The newer audience segments, youth and affluents, were believed to be influenced by newer-style marketing tactics. Women were gaining power across industry segments, but tactics for reaching them was a mix derived from traditional and nontraditional media. The general public is still being reached through mass channels of television, radio, and sports marketing.

Arts and entertainment will grow in importance as a tactic, but its adoption rate is likely to remain slow, because there are fewer clear pathways to using those ties. As demand increases, this may prove to be an area of great experimentation and creativity.

Bibliography

Anderson, C.A., and D.G. Whitehouse. 1995. *New Thought: A Practical American Spirituality.* New York: Crossroads Publishing Company, Inc.

Anderson, Chris, and D. G. Whitehouse. 2006. *The Long Tail: Why the Future of Business Is Selling Less of More.* New York: Hyperion Publishing Company, Inc.

Anonymous. 1997. *Lives and Works in the Arts: From the Renaissance to the 20th Century, Volume I.* Armonk, NY: M.E. Sharpe, Inc.

Aretino, Pietro. Il primo libro delle lettere, letter #162 to Ferrieri Beltramo.

Arnheim, Rudolph. 1974. *Art and Visual Perception: A Psychology of the Creative Eye.* Berkeley: University of California Press.

———. 1969. *Visual Thinking.* Berkeley: University of California Press.

Associated Press. 2006. "Redford: Sundance a Bit Too Intense," Kdka .com. February 16.

———. 2006. "Undergraduate Survey: iPods More Popular than Beer."

http://www.mercurynews.com/mld/mercurynews/news/breaking_news/ 14764223.htm. June 7.

Ashman, Helen, guest ed. 2002. "Special Issue on Hypermedia and the World Wide Web," *The New Review of Hypermedia and Multimedia*, vol. 8. http://www.comp.glam.ac.uk (retrieved May 6, 2006).

Avedon, Elliott, and Brian Sutton-Smith, eds. 1971. *The Study of Games.* New York: John Wiley & Sons.

Bakke, Dennis W. 2005. *Joy at Work.* Seattle: PVG.

Baron, Hans. 1966. *The Crisis of the Early Italian Renaissance.* Princeton, NJ: Princeton University Press.

Bergonzi, Louis, and Julia Smith. 1996. *Effects of Arts Education on Participation in the Arts.* Washington, DC: National Endowment for the Arts.

Bergson, Henri. 1961 [1909]. "The Individual and the Type," in *A Modern Books of Esthetics: An Anthology,* 3rd edition, ed. Melvin Rader. New York: Holt, Rinehart and Winston, pp. 80–87.

Bianchi, Marina. 2002. "Novelty, Preferences, and Fashion: When Good Things Are Unsettling," *Journal of Economic Behavior and Organization,* 47: 1–18.

Bianchini, Franco. 1993. "Remaking European Cities: The Role of Cultural Policies," in *Cultural Policy and Urban Regeneration,* ed. Franco Bianchi and Michael Parkinson. New York: Manchester University Press, pp. 1–20.

Biskind, Peter. 2004. *Down and Dirty Pictures.* New York: Simon & Schuster.

Bloom, B.S. 1963. "Report on Creativity Research by the Examiner's Office at the University of Chicago," in *Scientific Creativity: Its Recognition and Development,* ed. C.W. Taylor & F. Barron. New York: Wiley & Sons.

Booth, Wayne. 1988. *The Company We Keep: An Ethics of Fiction.* Berkeley and Los Angeles: University of California Press.

Bourdieu, Pierre. 1984. *Distinction: A Social Critique of Judgment of Taste.* Cambridge, MA: Harvard University Press.

Bradsher, Keith, and David Barboza. 2006. "Pollution from Chinese Coal Cast Shadow Around Globe," *New York Times.* June 11.

Bramante, Peter. 2006. Telephone interview. April 27.

Bransford, John D. 1979. *Human Cognition: Learning, Understanding, and Remembering.* Belmont, CA: Wadsworth Publishing Company.

Brockman, John. 1995. *The Third Culture.* New York: Simon & Schuster.

Brooks, Arthur C., and Roland J. Kushner. 2001. "Cultural Policy and Urban Development," *International Journal of Arts Management* 3, no. 2: 4–15.

Brooks, David. 2000. *Bobos in Paradise: The New Upper Class and How They Got There.* New York: Simon & Schuster.

Bryan, John. 2006. Phone interview. June 17.

Budd, Malcolm. 1995. *Values of Art.* London: Penguin Books.

California Arts Council. 2001. *Current Research in Arts Education: An Arts in Education Research Compendium.* Los Angeles: ARTS, Inc.

Cap Gemini. 2005. Collaboration Work. http://www.us.capgemini.com

Carroll, Noel. 2001. *Beyond Aesthetics: Philosophical Essays.* Cambridge, MA: Cambridge University Press.

Castronova, Edward. 2001. "Virtual Worlds: A First-Hand Account of Market and Society on the Cyberian Frontier," *CESifo Working Paper Series No. 618.* http://papers.ssrn.com/sol3/papers.cfm?abstract_id=294828

Catterall, James S. 1999. "Involvement in the Arts and Human Development: General Involvement and Intensive Involvement in Music and Theatre Arts," *Champions of Change.*

Chambers, J.A. 1964. "Relating Personality and Biographical Factors to Scientific Creativity." *Psychological Monographs* 78, no. 7 (Whole No. 584).

Chicago Loop Alliance. 2006. http://www.chicagoloopalliance.com. May 5.

Chicago Public Library. 2006. http://www.chipublib.org. June 4.

Collingwood, Robin George. 1958. *The Principles of Art.* New York: Oxford University Press.

Collins, Jim. 2001. *Good to Great.* New York: HarperCollins.

Copeland, Lee. 2000. "Development 2000: Good urban design reflects the essence of a community." http://www.djc.com. August 10.

Coppo Stefani Marchione di. 1370. *Florentine Chronicle, Rerum Italicarum.*

Crawford, Fred, and M. Ryan. 2001. *The Myth of Excellence.* New York: Cap, Gemini, Ernst and Young, US, LCC.

Creamer, Elizabeth G., and Lisa R. Lattuca. 2005. *Advancing Learning through Interdisciplinary Collaboration.* Hoboken, NJ: Wiley Periodicals, Inc.

Crow, Kelly. 2006. "Hot Art Market Stokes Prices for Artists Barely of Teens." *Wall Street Journal.* April 17.

Csikszentmihalyi, Mihaly. 1995. *Creativity: Flow and the Psychology of Discovery and Invention.* New York: HarperCollins.

———. 1990. *Flow.* New York: Harper and Row Publishers, Inc.

Cuno, James, ed. 2004. *Whose Muse? Art Museums and the Public Trust.* Princeton, NJ: Princeton University Press, and Cambridge, MA: Harvard University Art Museums.

Davis, Erik. TechGnosis: 1999. *Myth, Magic and Mysticism in the Age of Information.* New York: Three Rivers Press.

De Rosa, Cathy, L. Dempsey, and A. Wilson. 2003. *The 2003 OCLC Environmental Scan: Pattern Recognition.* Dublin: OCLC.

Dewey, John. 1980 [1934]. *Art as Experience.* New York: The Berkeley Publishing Company, Perigee Books.

Diamond, Jared. 2005. *Collapse*. London: Penguin Books.

——. 1999. *Guns, Germs, and Steel*. New York: W.W. Norton.

Dietrich, W. 2004. "Meet Your New Central Library." *Seattle Times.* April 25.

DiMaggio, Paul. 1996. "Are Museum Visitors Different From Other People? The Relationship Between Attendance and Social and Political Attitudes in the United States," *Poetics* 24: 161–80.

DPD. 2006. Population & Demographics Home: Seattle's Official Census Site. City of Seattle. June 14. http://www.seattle.gov/dpd/demographics

Durning, Alan. 2006. *Biography*. Sightline Institute. June 14.

Eaton, Nick. 2006. "Booming Development Set to Change Seattle's Look," *Seattle Post-Intelligencer.* http://seattlepi.nwsource.com/business/273888_downtown14.html. June 14.

Eberhart, Mark E. 2003. *Why Things Break.* New York: Harmony Books

Einstein, Albert, and Infeld, Leopold. 1938. *The Evolution of Physics.* Simon & Schuster.

Eisner, Elliot. 1972. *Educating Artistic Vision.* New York: Macmillan Company.

Elliott, G.R. 1938. *Humanism and Imagination.* New York: Kennikat Press, Inc.

Epstein, Richard A. 2003. "The Regrettable Necessity of Contingent Valuation," *Journal of Cultural Economics* 27: 259–74.

Florida, Richard. 2002. *The Rise of the Creative Class.* New York: Basic Books.

Friedman, Thomas L. 2005. *The World is Flat.* New York: Farrar, Strauss and Giroux.

Funch, Bjarne Sode. 1997. *The Psychology of Art Appreciation.* Copenhagen: University of Copenhagen.

Geyl, Pieter, P. A. Sorokin, and A. J. Toynbee. 1949. *The Pattern of the Past.* Boston: Boston Press.

Gilbert, Felix. 1980. *The Pope, His Banker, and Venice.* Cambridge, MA: Harvard University Press.

Gladwell, Malcolm. 2000. *The Tipping Point.* New York: Time Warner Book Group.

———. 2005. *Blink.* New York: Little, Brown and Company.

Gore, Al. 2006. "The Moment of Truth." *Vanity Fair.* May.

Grielsamer, Marc. 2006. *Review. Amazon.com.* June 25.

Gypsycabproject.com. July 1, 2006.

Halliwell, Sarah, ed. 1997. *Lives and Works in the Arts: From the Renaissance to the 20th Century,* Vol. 1. M.E. Sharpe.

Hamblem, Karen A. 1993. "Theories and Research that Support Art Instruction for Instrumental Outcomes," *Theory into Practice* 32, no. 4: 191–98.

Harlen, Wynne, and Craig Altobello. 2003. *An Investigation of "Try Science" Studied Online and Face-to-Face.* Cambridge, MA: TERC.

Harris, Neil. 1990. *Cultural Excursions.* Chicago: University of Chicago Press.

Harris, S. 2005. *The End of Faith.* New York: W.W. Norton & Company

Hayes, John R. 1990. *Cognitive Processes in Creativity.* Pittsburgh, PA: Carnegie Mellon University.

Hayes, J.R. 1978. *Cognitive Psychology: Thinking and Creating.* Homewood, IL: Dorsey Press.

———. 1985. "Thinking and Learning Skills: Research and Open Questions." In S. Chipman & R. Glaser (eds.), *Three Problems in Teaching Problem Solving Skills.*

Heinz, K. 1994. *The Incomplete History of Slam.* E-poets.net.

Herz, J. C. 1997. *Joystick Nation: How Videogames Ate Our Quarters, Won Our Hearts, and Rewired Our Minds.* New York: Little Brown.

Hill, Sam, and C. Lederer. 2001. *The Infinite Asset.* Cambridge, MA: Harvard Business School Press.

Holmes, George. 1986. *Florence, and the Origins of the Renaissance.* Oxford, UK: Oxford University Press.

Horrowitz, S. et al. 2006. "Creative Workers Count: New York City's Arts Funding Overlooks Individual Artists' Needs." *Freelancers Union Report.*

Howe, Neil, and W. Strauss. 1997. *The Fourth Turning.* New York: Broadway Books.

———. 2000. *Millenials Rising.* New York: Random House.

Huizinga, John. 1950. *Homo Ludens: A Study of the Play Element in Culture.* Boston: Beacon Press.

IEG. 2006. "The Death of Demographics: Reebok's New Way of Looking at Consumers." *IEG Sponsorship Report Volume 25.* April 17.

International Monetary Fund. September, 2006. *World Economic Outlook: Growth and Institutions.* www.imf.org.

Jacobs, Jane. 1961. *The Death and Life of American Cities.* New York: Random House.

Jensen, Rolf. 1999. *The Dream Society: How the Coming Shift from Information to Imagination Will Transform Your Business.* Columbus, OH: McGraw-Hill.

Juniper, Andrew. 2003. *Wabi-Sabi.* Boston: Tuttle Publishing.

Kaufman, Antony. 2006. "indieWIRE's Undistributed Gems Launches Tonight with *Chain*—Will Anyone Be There?" *Blogs.indiewire.com.* April 25.

Kelly, John R., 1987. *Freedom to be Me: A New Sociology of Leisure.* New York: Macmillan.

Kelly, John R., and Valeria J. Freysinger. 2000. *21st-Century Leisure: Current Issues.* Boston: Allyn and Bacon.

Kent, Steven L. 2001. *The Ultimate History of Video Games: From Pong to Pokemon and Beyond—The Story Behind the Craze that Touched Our Lives and Changed the World.* New York: Prima.

King, Geoff, and Tanya Kryzywinska. 2002. *Screen Play: Cinema/Videogames/Interfaces.* London: Wallflower.

King, Ross. 2003. *Michelangelo and the Pope's Ceiling.* New York: Walker Publishing Company.

Klosterman, Chuck. 2006. "The DJ Auteur." *The New York Times.* June 18.

Kolbert, E. 2001. "Pimps and Dragons: How an Online World Survived a Social Breakdown." *The New Yorker* 77, no. 3 (May 28): 88.

Kopznski, Mary, Mark Hager, and the Urban Institute. 2003. *The Value of the Performing Arts in Five Communities.* Philadelphia: The Pew Charitable Trusts.

Koren, Leonard. 1994. *Wabi-Sabi for Artists, Designers, Poets, & Philosophers.* Berkeley, CA: Stone Bridge Press.

Kostner, Jaclyn. 2001. *Bionic Teamwork.* Chicago: Dearborn Trade.

Kotkin, Joel, and Ross C. DeVol. 2001. *Knowledge-Value Cities in the Digital Age.* Santa Monica, CA: Milken Institute.

Kotler, Neil, and P. Kolter. 1998. *Museum Strategy and Marketing.* Hoboken, NJ: Jossey-Bass Publishers.

Levinson, Jarold. 2003. *The Oxford Handbook of Aesthetics.* Oxford, UK: Oxford University Press.

Lewis, Richard W. 1996. *Absolut Book.* Boston: Journey Editions.

Lindstrom, Martin. 2005. *Brand Sense: Build Powerful Brands through Touch, Taste, Smell, Sight, and Sound.* New York: Free Press.

Machiavelli, Niccolo. 2005. *The Prince.* New York: Bedford/St. Martin's.

Manovich, Lev. 2001. *The Language of New Media.* Cambridge, MA: MIT Press.

Mansfield, Richard S., and Thomas V. Busse. 1981. *The Psychology of Creativity and Discovery.* Nelson-Hall.

McCarthy, Kevin, E. Ondaatje, L. Zakaras, and A. Brooks. *Gifts of the Muse.* New York: Rand Corporation.

Mook, Douglas. 2004. *Classic Experiments in Psychology.* New York: Greenwood Press.

Murray, Janet. 2000. *Hamlet on the Holodeck: The Future of Narrative in Cyperspace.* Cambridge, MA: MIT Press.

Museum of Science and Industry. 2006. Exhibition didactic signage, Chicago, April.

Naisbitt, John. 1982. *Megatrends.* New York: Warner Books, Inc.

National Assembly of State Arts Agencies (NASAA). 1997. *Measuring Your Arts Economy: Twelve Questions and Answers about Economic Impact Studies.*

National Endowment for the Arts. 2003. *2002 Survey of Public Participation in the Arts, NEA Research Division Note 81.* Washington, DC: National Endowment for the Arts.

Nellams, Robert. 2005. "Seattle Center—What a Great Place!" City of Seattle. http://www.seattlecenter.com/default.asp

Newport, F. 2006. "A Look at Religious Switching in America Today: Majority of Americans Keep the Same Religion They've Always Had." Retrieved on June 23 from Gallup.com. http://poll.gallup.com/content/default.aspx?ci=23467&pg=1

New Yorker Magazine and LaPlaca Cohen. 2005. Culture Counts Study.

Noonan, Douglas S. 2003. "Contingent Valuation and Cultural Resources: A Meta-analytic Review of the Literature," *Journal of Cultural Economics* 27: 159–76.

Nozick, Robert. 1981. *Philosophical Explanations.* Boston: Belknap Press.

Oblinger, Diana. 2003. "Boomers, Gen-Xers, and Millenials: Understanding the 'New Students,'" *EDUCAUSE Review* 38, no. 4 (July/August): 37–47.

OCLC. 2003. OCLC Environmental Scan, 2003. OCLC.org.

Ortiz, Benjamin. 2001. "Free Verse Fight Club: Do-It-Yourself Organizing at the San Antonio Poetry Slam," *Punk Planet Magazine.* February.

Pearson, Carol S. 1989. *The Hero Within.* New York: Harper and Row Publishers, Inc.

Performance Research, Ltd. 1997. Performance Research Study of Arts and Culture Sponsorship.

Pine II, B. Joseph, and J. H. Gilmore. 1999. *The Experience Economy.* Cambridge, MA: Harvard Business School Press.

Pink, Daniel H. 2005. *A Whole New Mind: Moving from the Information Age to the Conceptual Age.* New York: Penguin Group, Inc.

———. 2001. *Free Agent Nation.* New York: Warner Books, Inc.

———. 2005. "The New Power Generation." *Wired,* issue 13.05, May.

Plotnik, Arthur. 1996. *The Elements of Expression.* New York: Henry Holt and Company, Inc.

Poole, Steven. 2000. *Trigger Happy: Video Games and the Entertainment Revolution.* New York: Arcade.

Popcorn, Faith, and Lys Marigold. 2001. *EVEolution: Understanding Women—Eight Essential Truths that Work in Your Business and in Your Life.* New York: Hyperion.

Postrel, Virginia. 2003. *The Substance of Style.* New York: HarperCollins.

Ray, P. H., and S. R. Anderson. 2001. *Cultural Creatives: How 50 Million People Are Changing the World.* Victoria, BC, Canada: Crown Publications.

Robertson, Campbell. 2006. "THEATRE: We All Got Together and Put On a Brand." *New York Times,* July 2.

Ryan, Marie-Laure. 2001. *Narrative and Virtual Reality: Immersion and Interactivity in Literature and Electronic Media.* Baltimore: Johns Hopkins Press.

Salen, Katie, and Eric Zimmerman. 2004. *Rules of Play: Game Design Fundamentals.* Cambridge, MA: MIT Press.

Salzmen, Mary, Chris Dede, R. Bowen Loftin, and Jim Chen. 1999. "A Model for Understanding How Virtual Reality Aids Complex Conceptual Learning," *Presence: Teleoperators and Virtual Environments* 8, no. 3 (May): 293–316.

Schonberg, H. C. 1970. *The Lives of Great Composers.* New York: W.W. Norton & Co.

Seattle Public Library. 2006. http://www.spl.org. June 14.

Seifter, Harvey, and P. Economy. 2001. *Leadership Ensemble.* New York: Henry Holt and Company, LLC.

Sims, Patterson. "Scuola de Chihuly: Venezia and Seattle." Dale Chihuly, Inc. *www.chihuly.com/essays/scuola.html.*

Sitwell, Nigel. 1981. *Roman Roads of Europe.* New York: St. Martin's Press.

Sloan, James Allen. 2002. *The Romance of Commerce and Culture: Capitalism, Modernization, and the Chicago-Aspen Crusade for Cultural Reform.* Boulder: University Press of Colorado.

Smith, Dinitia. 2006. "In the Age of the Overamplified, a Resurgence for the Humble Lecture." *New York Times,* March 17.

Smuts, Aaron. 2005. *Occasional Paper: Video Games and the Philosophy of Art.* American Society for Aesthetics, aesthetics-online.org.

Snider, M. 2002. "Where Movies End, Games Begin; Industry Mimics Studio Techniques and Profitability." *USA Today,* May 23, p. D03.

Sobel, David. 2002. "Beyond Ecophobia: Reclaiming the Heart in Nature Education." *Orion Society Nature Literacy Series.*

Sorokin, Pitirim A. 1964. *The Basic Trends of Our Times.* New York: College and University Press Services, Inc.

———. 1928. *Contemporary Sociological Theories.* New York: Harper and Row Publishers, Inc.

———. 1941. *The Crisis of Our Age.* New York: E.P. Dutton and Co., Inc.

———. 1938. *Social and Cultural Dynamics.* American Book Company.

Squire, K.D., and C.A. Steinkuehler. 2004. "The Culture of Play." Paper presented as the State of Play Conference, New York University Law School, New York. October 28–31.

Steinhart, Peter. 2004. *The Undressed Art: Why We Draw.* New York: Alfred A. Knopf.

Steinkuehler, C. A. 2005. *Styles of Play: Gamer-Identified Trajectories of Participation in MMOGs.* Paper presented at Annual Conference of the Digital Games Research Association (DIGRA), Vancouver, June 16–20.

————. 2005. Cognition and Learning in Massively Multiplayer Online Games: A Critical Approach. Unpublished dissertation for the University of Wisconsin–Madison.

Surowiecki, James. 2004. *The Wisdom of Crowds: Why Many are Smaller than the Few and How Collective Wisdom Shapes Business, Economics, Societies, and Nations.* New York: Doubleday.

Tapscott, Don. 1998. *Growing Up Digital: The Rise of the Net Generation.* New York: McGraw Hill.

Taylor, Charles. 1989. *Sources of the Self: The Making of the Modern Identity.* Cambridge, MA: Harvard University Press.

Taylor, Jim, and Watts Wacker. 1997. *The 500-Year Delta: What Happens after What Comes Next.* New York: Harper Business Books.

Tchong, Michael. 2004. *Trendscapes 2004.* San Francisco: Trendscape.

Tharp, Twyla, with M. Reiter. 2003. *The Creative Habit.* New York: Simon & Shuster.

Thompson, A. 2005. *Cities of God: The Religion of Italian Communes, 1125–1325.* State College, PA: Penn State Univ. Press.

Throsby, C. David. 2004. "Assessing the Impacts of a Cultural Industry." Paper prepared for Lasting Effects: Assessing the Future of Economic Impact Analysis Conference. Tarrytown, NY. May.

Toffler, Alvin. 1970. *Future Shock.* New York: Bantam Books.

Trendwatching.com. May 12, 2006.

Underhill, Pace. 1999. *Why We Buy: The Science of Shopping.* New York: Simon & Schuster.

U.S. National Institute for Technology & Liberal Education. 2004. *BlogCensus.* Blogcensus.net. June.

Van Gelder, Lawrence. 2006. "Arts, Briefly." *New York Times.* July 3.

Villani, Fillipo. 1857. *Cronica* 8, no. 26. Trieste, Italy.

von Neumann, John. 2000. *The Computer and the Brain*. New Haven, CT: Yale University Press.

Walker, Paul Robert. 2002. *The Feud that Sparked the Renaissance*. New York: HarperCollins.

Wallace Foundation. 2005. "RAND Study Says Arts Policy Should Focus on Building Individual Appreciation of the Arts." *Wallacefoundation.org*. February 15.

———. 2004. "What the Arts Can Do for Me and My Community: An Analysis of a National Survey," study by Belden, Russanello, and Stewart. The Wallace Foundation and Culture Counts.

Welch, Evelyn. 1997. *Art and Society in Italy 1350–1500*. Oxford, UK: Oxford University Press.

Wheelan, Susan A. 1999. *Creating Effective Teams*. London: Sage Publishing.

Whitmont, Edward C. 1982. *Return of the Goddess*. New York: Crossroad.

Wolf, Mark J. P. 2001. *The Medium of the Video Game*. Austin: UT Press.

Wolf, Mark J. P., and Bernard Perron, eds. 2003. *The Video Game Theory Reader*. New York: Routledge.

Ypma, E. G. 1970. "Predictions of the Industrial Creativity of Research Scientists from Biographical Information." Doctoral dissertation, Purdue University, 1968. *Dissertation Abstracts International* 30, no. 5731B-5732B.

Index